CORAL GABLES

THE CITY BEAUTIFUL STORY

CORAL GABLES

THE CITY BEAUTIFUL STORY

by LES STANDIFORD

EDITOR, Rob Levin
EDITORIAL ASSOCIATE, Cheryl Sadler
PROJECT MANAGEMENT, Jan Pogue and Anne Murdoch
CORAL GABLES LIAISON, Raena Alexis Latina
NEW PHOTOGRAPHY, Alan S. Maltz and Ken Hawkins
BOOK & JACKET DESIGN AND COMPOSITION, Karen Smith of Stateless Design
COPYEDITING & INDEXING, Bob Land

CORAL GABLES CHAMBER BOOK COMMITTEE:
Ronald W. Robison, President/CEO, Coral Gables Chamber
Raena Alexis Latina, Director of Communications, Coral Gables Chamber
Connie Crowther, Crowther & Company Communications & Consulting
Danette Gossett, Gossett Marketing Communications

CORAL GABLES CHAMBER OF COMMERCE
50 Aragon Avenue
Coral Gables, FL 33134-5372
Phone: 305-446-1657
Fax: 305-446-9900

Book Development:
RIVERBEND BOOKS, LTD.
501 Means Street, Suite B
Atlanta, GA 30318
Phone: 404-681-0909

ISBN: 1-883987-04-0
First Edition

Printed in Korea

THE CORAL GABLES CHAMBER OF COMMERCE, FLORIDA CHAMBER OF COMMERCE EXECUTIVES 1997 "CHAMBER OF THE YEAR," IS A PRIVATE, NONPROFIT ORGANIZATION WHICH UNITES HUNDREDS OF BUSINESSES AND PROFESSIONAL FIRMS FOR NETWORKING, BUSINESS PROMOTION, SPECIAL EVENTS, AND THE BETTERMENT OF THE COMMUNITY.

AT THE GABLES CHAMBER, WE DON'T JUST TALK ABOUT THE FUTURE—WE SHAPE IT. OUR MISSION IS: "TO FOSTER AND ENHANCE THE ECONOMIC INTERESTS AND QUALITY OF LIFE IN THE CORAL GABLES COMMUNITY." OUR PROFESSIONAL STAFF AND A HOST OF VOLUNTEERS WORK TO SUPPORT THIS MISSION.

WE ARE PROUD TO HAVE ENVISIONED AND PUBLISHED *Coral Gables—The City Beautiful Story* TO SHOWCASE OUR WONDERFUL CITY.

This book is dedicated to the memory of George Merrick

and to the many citizens of Coral Gables who have carried his vision forward.

Acknowledgments

Many individuals deserve credit for making this book possible: their generous help and advice have been invaluable. The best of what is to be found here derives from the contributions of others; any errors and omissions are mine. Profound thanks to: Ellen J. Uguccioni, director of the Coral Gables Department of Historic Preservation; Ron Robison, president of the Coral Gables Chamber of Commerce; Raena A. Latina, director of communications for the Chamber; Carol R. McGeehan, curator of Coral Gables Merrick House; Joe Keefe, video production manager of Coral Gables TV; Cathy Swanson, Coral Gables Director of Development; Professor Marvin Dunn of Florida International University; Al Linero, director of public works for the city of Coral Gables; Connie Crowther of Crowther & Company Communications & Consulting; Danette Gossett, Gossett Marketing Communications; Alvin Cassell of Broad & Cassell; Bill Wagner, manager of the Riviera Country Club; Donald Kuhn; Marge Hartnett; Helen Muir; Gary and Cynthia McGraw of Gili-McGraw Architects; Professor William Brown, director of special collections at the University of Miami Richter Library; Stephanie Kirby, director of public relations for the Biltmore Hotel; Mitch Kaplan of Books & Books; Dick Shaw for the use of his boat; Michael Freeman for his attention to the legal details; Samuel D. LaRoue Jr. for the use of his wonderful postcard collection; and to all the others who have been so kind.

LES STANDIFORD
Coral Gables, Florida
February 1998

"...all human endeavor must first contribute to the furtherance of that supreme wealth of the people, life in abundance. That is what Coral Gables does."

MARJORY STONEMAN DOUGLAS

Contents

Foreword

By Ronald W. Robison, President/CEO, Coral Gables Chamber of Commerce

Opportunities and Challenges!—Many cities in Dade County and around the nation have what is commonly referred to as 'coffee table' books about their city. As unlikely as it may seem, Coral Gables, with all of its history, rich heritage and beauty, does not have a 'coffee table' book. There are several small books about our community and about George Merrick, but not one large pictorial book about Coral Gables.

"I'm looking for someone to champion this cause, form an ad hoc committee, and produce a book about our City Beautiful. Please give me a call to discuss any interest you may have in this project."

The foregoing is excerpted from my "President's Report" of February 1996. Fortunately, I had two of our Chamber members respond to my request. Connie Crowther and Danette Gossett stepped forward to work with Chamber Director of Communications Raena A. Latina and me. *Coral Gables—The City Beautiful Story* would not have become a reality without Connie and Danette—I will be forever grateful to them for their sincere interest and dedication to this project. Raena was the task force coordinator, keeping us focused and on schedule by setting up appointments as well as sharing her knowledge and giving input to the project by virtue of her Masters in Communication from the University of Miami.

All of us agreed at the outset that this would be a storybook about a man, his dreams, and a city. A

ABOVE: Coral Gables Chamber of Commerce President Ron Robison. LEFT: The facade of Merrick Place, the city's recently constructed multi-use parking structure. The building houses ground-level shops and a bicycle police substation as well as 430 parking spaces. Its attractive design, landscaping, and sculpture sometimes confuses motorists: city officials erected additional signage to make clear that the building is indeed a parking garage.

man unlike any other man of his time, with dreams of a city unlike any other city of its time. Interestingly enough, George Merrick's dream of Coral Gables materialized over a period of years as he grew up from a young boy arriving in Florida at age twelve to a man of thirty-eight when Coral Gables was incorporated. George must have somehow sensed the great potential this vast flatland had, and was able to convince many others to share in his vision.

(Incidentally, George arrived here in 1898—this book was published exactly one hundred years after his arrival. We on the "Book Committee" like to say it took one hundred years to create a book fitting for Coral Gables.)

Of course, George had no way of knowing the two significant external forces—the Cuban Revolution and the city's proximity to a major international airport—that would help shape his "dream city" into what it is today. Fortunately, Coral Gables was positioned to take advantage of these forces and, over the last four decades, has truly become a "Global City," as predicted in 1977 by the *Harvard Business Review.*

As you read this book—and I do hope that you read it and not just look at the pretty pictures—I would like to invite you to put on George's hat and shoes and see his vision, realize his successes and failures, and acknowledge that Coral Gables is what it is today because of this one man's dream.

CITY HALL, CORAL GABLES, FLORIDA

Golf and Country Club, Coral Gables, Miami, Fla.—66

CASCADES, VENETIAN POOL, CORAL GABLES, FLORIDA

Toledo Street, Coral Gables, Miami, Fla.

M7:—DE SOTO PLAZA AND MIAMI BILTMORE HOTEL, CORAL GABLES, FLA.

PART ONE

Ten-Mile Drive

EVERY CITY HAS ITS concrete spinal column, the route that travels its essential core. Maybe it's a long, unbroken boulevard like Figueroa Street in Los Angeles, Broadway in New York, or the Champs-Elysées in Paris; or perhaps it's a series of connectors like Roman byways, straining to make contact like those famous fingers on the ceiling of the Sistine Chapel. But long or short, unbroken or spliced, it is essential to find that corridor, that route along the spine where, the city's nerve center runs. Travel that route a few times, you come to appreciate the place in a way you couldn't in any other fashion.

The route I trace through Coral Gables is my own, admittedly, appearing on no guide book or official map. It is not the length of thirty-mile-long Figueroa Street, say, not by a long shot: only 10.3 miles from end to end, and that could probably be shaved a bit if someone else designed the route. Nor does it compare in age or legend to those golden boulevards of Europe such as the Champs-Elysées and the Via Veneto. Even the street names change half a dozen times along the way. But the diversity this route stitches is as complex as any, and as for scenic richness, it beats them all, hands down.

I last drove it on a steamy July weekday at midmorning when traffic promised to be light, beginning at the southern-most terminus of Red Road. Red, by the way, is one of the few

LEFT: Some of the most stunning new homes in Coral Gables are found along its myriad waterways. BELOW: George Merrick didn't miss much when planning his city—even arranging for these vans to transport potential lot buyers from Miami.

unexotically titled streets in Coral Gables; along with its cousin Blue Road, the pair are holdovers from the practice of government surveyors who would typically lay out the principal north-south roadways of virgin territory in red, their east-west intersectors in blue.

As it happens now, Red Road dead ends at an extension of SW 136th Street. There is a solid mass of mangroves blocking the way, an unbroken tangle that constitutes the principal feature of an untended square mile or so of coastal wetlands referred to on the Coral Gables map as Chapman Field Park.

A bit to the west, some of these impassable lowlands have been reclaimed: make a long roundabout detour and you'll come upon the upscale development of Deering Bay. Sprawling about an Arnold Palmer-designed golf course, Deering Bay lies less than a quarter mile away, as the gull flies. There are also a couple of public ball fields over that way, giving some substance to the area's designation as a park. But here, in this section, things look much as they must have when the settlers arrived in earnest in South Florida, a century and a quarter ago.

I pull over and step out into the summer heat, noting the background din of cicadas and greenhouse frogs (the size of your thumb, these natives of Cuba can rival the bullfrog in volume). There's a footpath tunneling eastward through the mangroves and I decide to give it a shot, a couple hundred yards of slip-sliding through the tidal flats and across driftwood bridges fashioned by adventurous children, until even that track peters out atop a foot-high knob of coral surrounded by the spidery roots of mangroves. There is a glistening bay out there somewhere, I

know, but here there are only the low-lying mangroves, the mudflats, the tide-puddles, the crabholes, and the occassional whine of mosquitoes—in short, things are pretty much as they were when Coral Gables was just a dream.

The lower half of this writer's route cuts through the Riviera section of the city, so designated by George Merrick, the city's founder, who once envisioned a South Florida version of the Cote d'Azur on these six thousand or more shoreside acres he added to his development's original bounds back in the 1920s. Some of Merrick's most fanciful dreams were planned for this area, though most would die aborning, and he himself would not live to see what finally transpired here. Most of the Riviera District was to lay undeveloped for many years; it was well into the 1950s before the area began to take its present form.

From its southernmost point, stolidly named Red Road runs due north, the flanking mangrove tangle soon giving way to the manicured lawns of Gables by the Sea, one of many luxurious but modern developments.

There's a short detour here, a jog around a newly erected traffic barrier near the entrance to Gulliver Academy, which with its two thousand students is the largest of Dade County's private schools. Gulliver, founded and still directed by Marian Krutulis, began its life in the adjacent community of Coconut Grove in the early 1950s, then moved to its present twenty-acre site in 1967, eventually growing so busy that traffic has had to be rerouted to keep commuters moving along the nearby arteries.

From Gulliver, it's another half mile or so along Red Road, past the enclave of Pine Bay Estates on the west, and the fenced, 120-acre estate of The Montgomery

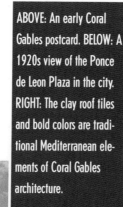

ABOVE: An early Coral Gables postcard. BELOW: A 1920s view of the Ponce de Leon Plaza in the city. RIGHT: The clay roof tiles and bold colors are traditional Mediterranean elements of Coral Gables architecture.

Foundation on the East. The latter, now a world-renowned palm and cycad research center, was once the home of Colonel Robert Montgomery and his wife, Nell. Montgomery, who was born the son of a Methodist minister in 1872 and who never set foot inside a college class-room as a student, but went on to become a storied professor of business at Colum-bia University and to found one of the most successful accounting firms in the country.

In later life, Montgomery was to take an interest in plant collecting, and in the early 1930s purchased an estate in Coconut Grove, a place he called the Palmetum, where he developed a collection of palms and cycads that soon overwhelmed the available acreage. This shortage of space led to the purchase of the southerly Gables tract where he and Nell lived for many years, and was to result as well in the for-mation of Fairchild Tropical Garden, yet another Coral Gables landmark.

To reach this treasure, one must turn right off Red Road and wind northeastward along scenic Old Cutler Road, so named for a Massachusetts pioneer who developed a fruit and vegetable farm further south in the 1880s and used the trail to truck his produce into Coconut Grove. Along the venerable way is the Doris and Phil Sanford Fire Station, tucked amongst the pines on the right, itself the focus of some notoriety and further Montgomery philanthropy. No such firehouse

BELOW LEFT: The annual Ramble at Fairchild Tropical Garden draws thousands to one of the largest festivals in South Florida. RIGHT: Visitors admire a thatched hut, constructed by native South American craftsmen, located on the grounds of the internationally acclaimed Fairchild Tropical Garden botanical preserve. The garden was founded by Robert Montgomery in 1938 and designed by William Lyman Phillips. A former CCC superintendent, Phillips designed all of the area's public parks, includ-ing Matheson Hammock, and is generally credited with the creation of the South Florida landscaping "look."

existed in these parts until a few years back; emer-gencies in the South Gables required the dispatch of vehicles from city stations nearly six miles to the north, or the sometimes unwieldy process of back-up from neighboring Dade County. Everyone agreed on the need for a station in the South Gables, but no one could settle on where to put it until the Montgomery Foundation stepped for-ward, providing what must be one of the more scenic fire station sites around.

Just past the station, one crosses the Snapper Creek Canal, part of the extensive South Florida water-management system. Pleasure boats and cabin cruisers bob the snug waters of Snapper Creek Marina just to the north and west of Old Cutler, while a glance in the opposite direction offers a rare peek all the way out to Biscayne Bay.

The canal cuts through a sizable chunk of state-owned, county-maintained land here, land that to the casual eye might seem in need of some careful tending and pruning. But the 820-acre tract is in fact existing much as intended: the R. Hardy Matheson Preserve, named after the former Metro Dade County commissioner, was once destined for hotel and golf course development by ITT, before environmental groups intervened. The land was purchased in the 1980s, using conservation and environmental funds, with the intent of making it look and function much the same way it did near the turn of the century.

BELOW AND RIGHT: The lushness, serenity, and beauty of the Fairchild Tropical Garden is evident everywhere within its borders. Rare flora from all over the world can be found, either via a walking or tram tour.

While the Matheson preserve still serves as an environmental buffer and site for nature walks, bird watching, and nature studies for the public (bald eagles, ospreys, and frigate birds fish there; and skunks, rabbits, racoons, opossums, grey foxes, and West Indian manatee also call the area home), no contrast could be greater between that vast area and the grounds that lay just to the north.

Shortly after the move to their South Gables estate, Montgomery and his wife were to extend their interest in tropical horticulture in a philanthropic direction, donating fifty-eight acres of nearby land for the creation of Fairchild Tropical Garden, where today more tropical plants grow than in any other spot in the mainland United States. The Garden, as it is often referred to, was named after David Fairchild, a friend of the Montgomery family and the creator and first director of the U.S. Department of Agriculture.

Dedicated in 1938, Fairchild Tropical Garden has grown to some eighty-three acres, serving as an international research center and attracting nearly one hundred thousand visitors annually to grounds so striking that best-selling author and poet David Rosenberg used them as the research model for an imaginative recreation of Eden and the Book of Genesis. The Garden serves its community in more ways as well: there are some six thousand members who not only visit regularly but who volunteer in myriad ways, offering tours and classes in gardening and aiding in the many plant sales and distributions that spread the Garden's bounty about the yards and gardens of the Gables and elsewhere in South Florida.

Just beyond Fairchild, Old Cutler begins a mile-long tunnel beneath the canopy of live oak and

banyan that makes driving so many of the Gables streets exotic. It's not so annoying to follow a slow-moving truck or plod along in rush-hour traffic when you're a mote in such an art-inspiring leafy artery, with time to appreciate the chiaroscuro of sun-

light and shade filtering down. The views are so striking that they have, along with similar vistas from Ingraham and Main Highways in neighboring Coconut Grove, become a staple of the local art scene.

Here, the shaded route bisects the grounds of Matheson Hammock Park, part of the Miami-Dade County system and the only seaside park in Coral Gables. The one-hundred-acre tract is the gift of another fabled Miami-area developer and philanthropist, Commodore W. J. Matheson, who deeded over the land in 1930. The spacious picnic grounds laid out beneath the live oaks are visible from the roadway, which is itself flanked by one of the more popular bike trails in the region. Further to the east is a sizable marina and a protected beach on a man-made lagoon, which is a special draw for toddler-equipped families year round.

There's also a singular feature about the concession facility that serves those family-oriented beach crowds. Like most others of its ilk, the place dutifully serves up hot dogs and chips and soft drinks during the daylight hours. But once the sun goes down, the beachside window is shuttered, tiki torches are lit, and the building transforms itself into an elegant, lagoonside restaurant.

The Red Fish Grill was the brainchild of longtime Gables restaurateur Mike Namour, co-owner of Christy's Restaurant, who had always longed to see a

seaside restaurant in his city. When Hurricane Andrew destroyed the existing concessions in the park, Namour convinced officials to give his unconventional plan a try as they rebuilt. "The last concessionaire used to recycle his grilled hot dogs for two or three days until they finally sold," Namour says. "I convinced the county we could do better than that, and that they'd get a nice restaurant besides." Whether drawn by the food or the striking nighttime views of the downtown skyline far across the bay, the crowds have indeed come to the only seaside restaurant in Coral Gables. George Merrick, who once envisioned so much night life in grand casinos and hotels on these shores, would surely approve.

North of Matheson, the land between Old Cutler and the sea is given over to some of the most elegant and most recently developed of Coral Gables neighborhoods, Gables Estates and Cocoplum among them. The lots are large, as are the homes, and nearly all front on the water. At the time of this writing, an average home in Cocoplum might sell for eight hundred thousand dollars. But, go a bit further eastward in that neighborhood, onto now-private

ABOVE: An aerial view of the lagoon of Matheson Hammock Park. LEFT: One of the chefs of the Red Fish Grill displays some of her culinary talents.
RIGHT: A 1950s view of the lagoon at Matheson Hammock Park, the only public beach in Coral Gables. The park looks much the same today and remains a popular spot for family outings.

The outdoor dining patio of the Red Fish Grill at Matheson Hammock overlooks the lagoon.

With the Miami skyline as a backdrop, a visitor to Matheson Hammock Park walks the beach which circles the lagoon. The protected swimming area makes it a safe water recreation site for children, as well as for afternoon lounging by adults.

Tahiti Island—where George Merrick once ferried prospects to a beachside nightclub—and you will discover an enclave within an enclave, where home prices soar to $4 million and $5 million and beyond.

One may come out of Cocoplum dizzied by all that grandeur, but that is no reason not to make a full circle around Cartagena Plaza, the traffic roundabout that fronts the entrance to the development. It's one of several such European-influenced plazas in Merrick's fanciful layout, and the one most recently developed. Taking the circle is the best way to appreciate the huge bronze sculpture of a pair of battered shoes sitting in the middle of the landscaped plaza. The sculpture was placed in 1979 as a gesture of friendship from Coral Gables's sister city of

RIGHT: A view of the Ferdinand Street Bridge in 1925, which was built across a dry river bed. The bridge is no longer there. LEFT: Tahiti Beach delivered what this postcard promised —a tropical isle setting. Of course, there was also dining and dancing. The area is now an upscale residential development. BELOW: Venetian gondolas and their gondoliers at Tahiti Beach, as it appeared in 1926. Biltmore Hotel guests seeking the seaside experience were ferried down the Coral Gables Waterway by pilots imported from Italy. While the route remains navigable, the craft and the beach are long gone: the latter has become the upscale development of Cocoplum.

Cartagena, Colombia. Hector Lombana, the sculptor, executed the piece as a mirror of his original piece in Cartagena, a monument to Colombian poet Luis Carlos Lopez. Lopez once wrote a tribute to his native city that concluded with the words: "You inspire the same love one may have for a pair of very comfortable old shoes," and in 1956 Lombana executed the original sculpture in lieu of a more formal appreciation. Later, during a visit to Miami, Lombana saw a tiny reproduction of his work that had been placed in the Gables plaza; dissatisfied with how it looked, the sculptor volunteered to create the piece that dominates the spacious roundabout today.

At the imaginary mile marker 4.9 of my mythical route, Cartagena Plaza marks a point of transition between old Gables and new. Northeastward-bearing Old Cutler Road leaves off here, giving over to Le Jeune Road, which runs due north. There is another landmark here as well:

just north of the Plaza a bridge spans the course of the Coral Gables Waterway, an artery that figured greatly in George Merrick's original plans. Though a child could toss a rock from bank to bank, and though it measures perhaps eight miles in length, including all its loops and turns, it might as well have been the Nile in its creator's mind.

Merrick, savvy enough to understand that Florida property, while attractive, would be even more attractive with access to the water, used gondolas crafted in Italy (and gondoliers from Venice) to ferry guests from the Biltmore Hotel down its twisting course to the bayside pleasure dome he'd fashioned at Tahiti Beach, at the southerly bank of the canal's mouth. Very important personages and prospects of the day lounged on the sands, dined at bayside, and stayed to dance the night away to the strains of Paul Whiteman's orchestra and others. Merrick envisioned a European-inspired casino on the point of land just

to the north, a second bayside, Biltmore Hotel close by and an enormous marina further south.

Shortly after he acquired the Riviera tract, Merrick had the boundaries of Coral Gables redrawn, to encompass not only his new waterfront acreage, but to actually reach out from the mainland and incorporate Key Biscayne on the north as well. At that time, Key Biscayne was a coconut plantation reachable only by boat, most of its land owned by pioneers W. J. Matheson and Charles Deering. While no property ever changed hands, Matheson and Deering did agree to the incorporation, most likely intrigued by Merrick's own success at transforming grapefruit groves into developer's gold.

From Key Biscayne, Merrick arranged his boundaries southward over the wavelets to Soldier Key, and from there back to land at Chapman Field, including all the sea bottom in between. He envisioned the creation of a series of islands formed by dredging up that encircled sea bottom, much as

This shot, taken outside the Casa Loma Hotel in 1925, is typical of the social swirl in the glory days of Merrick development. Note the original pine canopy visible in the background. The site of the Casa Loma is today part of the Biltmore Hotel's parking lot.

Carl Fisher had done in Miami Beach, these islands to be connected by Venetian-inspired bridges and forming a fairy-tale lacework to be viewed from a causeway running along the shore. The whole would constitute a scenic loop and series of exotic home sites that would outdo anything theretofore known, at least as Merrick conceived it.

"Forty miles of waterfront!" Merrick's promotional booklets began to boast, though certain critics sniffed in return: "Sure. Twenty miles up one side of those canals, twenty miles back down."

The islands were never dredged, the bridges, causeways, and casinos never built, of course. (Key Biscayne was to de-incorporate in the 1940s, shortly before a causeway was constructed to connect the island with the mainland and serious development began.) Little remains of Merrick's grander vision for the waterway and its intended network of pleasure palaces, inland marinas, and water parks.

But one legacy attached to the Coral Gables water- way has endured: the rugged limestone cliffs that

rise up twenty feet or more to abut the crossing beneath Le Jeune Road. Surely the only such geological feature within several hundred miles, the formation seems positively fjord-like in comparison to the pancake-flat surroundings. Visiting tour buses are drawn to the sight in droves.

There is also another aspect of that geological feature, though perhaps not so obvious, which holds far more dramatic implications for the area's ecology. For until this man-made gouge was blasted through the rock, its limestone barrier prevented the escape of fresh water out of the Everglades, or River of Grass, as Marjory Stoneman Douglas has called that vast ecosystem only a few miles west. Until the Coral Gables Waterway and many other such artificial cuts were made during the Florida boom years and after, fresh water flowing down from Lake Okechobee and beyond had been forced on southward

until it poured into Florida Bay at the very end of the continent. During periods of heavy rainfall, this meant considerable flooding at the western verge of the narrow habitable strip between ocean and Everglades.

Early developers sought to alleviate this inconvenience and extend the range of their pursuits by blasting and diverting directly to the ocean, a practice that continued well into the latter stages of the twentieth century. More land to develop, more

residents, more tax dollars, a healthier economy—
or so it seemed—and it seemed too good to be true.

Of course, it was. The diversion of fresh water
and the increase in agricultural and developmen-
tally related pollutants pouring into what is left of
the southward flow has led to a serious disruption
of the ecology of the Everglades, and in turn, to
that of Florida Bay, threatening wildlife, natural
reefs, shrimping and fishing, and most ominously,

(CONTINUED ON PAGE 45)

You're in the Gables, Now

The shin-high street signs in Coral Gables make for some interesting path finding—especially at night. ABOVE RIGHT: When this picture was taken of the Granada entrance, the current stone marker street signage was not in place; that didn't come until the 1940s.

S GREEN WAY
800

The intention of Denman Fink and George Merrick was that a visit to the city would begin with a passage through one of eight elaborately designed entrances intended to evoke the feeling of passing through the gates of an exotic walled city of antiquity. In addition to the Douglas, Commercial, Granada, and Country Club Prado Entrances, four others were planned but never built, including Bayside (proposed for the intersection of Coral Way and Douglas Road), Gladeside (Coral Way and Red Road), Coconut Grove (Douglas and Coconut Grove Drive), and Flagler (Flagler Street and Ponce de Leon Boulevard).

The existing entrances are indeed grand, and impossible to miss. But perhaps the most compelling signal for contemporary visitors that they have entered Gables territory is the appearance of the idiosyncratic, low-lying stone street markers dotting every intersection in the city. Most assume that the peculiar signage, commonly referred to by local residents as tombstones, is another legacy from the Merrick years, but such is not the case.

Merrick, in fact, used rustic wooden signage to mark his streets. The stone markers, evocative of stone mileage posts on the east-west National Highway (later U.S. 40) and elsewhere in the country, were an addition of the 1940s, when they were deployed in tandem with similarly styled, ground-hugging stop signs done in neon paint for nighttime visibility. "We finally had to get rid of the stop signs for safety reasons," says Al Linero, the city's longtime director of public works (one is still to be encountered, at the exit of the Merrick House parking lot). "And the county was after us there for a while to standardize everything. But we've managed to keep the street signs. People complain they can't find them or kids run over top of them and get high-centered, but they're part of the Gables, you know?"

And very durable besides. Linero scoffs when asked if the signs are vulnerable to theft. "They weigh about 250 pounds," he says. "Pretty tough to carry off."

The Greater Miami Symphonic Band performs during the Coral Gables annual Fourth of July Celebration, held on the grounds of the Biltmore golf course, which surrounds the Biltmore Hotel. The event, which attracts visitors from all over South Florida, includes appearances by the Congregational Church Chancel Choir and features one of the area's more extensive fireworks displays, using the famed Biltmore tower as a backdrop.

the underground aquifers that provide drinking water for every resident of South Florida. The threat has touched off a significant reorientation of priorities among residents and regulatory agencies, spawning any number of plans for revitalizing the Everglades and sparking a series of political battles that extend all the way to Washington, D.C. But one thing is certain: there will be no more corridors to the sea blasted through the caprock.

George Merrick, lover of nature and land, could not have conceived of such complications. He saw an opportunity to enhance the appeal of his city and the quality of life therein, and he seized it, doing only what other, far less principled developers had been doing for years. Today, one can only stand atop these lovely limestone cliffs and wonder if they'd have ever come into being if George

Merrick had realized fully the consequences of what he was doing.

The cut of the Coral Gables Waterway and Cartagena Plaza mark the southeast corner of the original Coral Gables plat. Guidebooks and pure esthetics might dictate a turn to the west at this point, to curve along Riviera Drive, past the lovely homes nestled on the north bank of the Waterway and into the heart of Old Gables beyond.

We might also opt for Granada Boulevard, which also soars away northwestward here, along an even grander course. It's a mile or so of impressive homes along the Waterway, then a quick leap past the site of the original Ponce de Leon High School (now a middle school) to cross U.S. Highway

LEFT: With the Biltmore tower hovering in the background, golfers test their putting skills on the Biltmore golf course's immaculate greens. RIGHT: A view from atop the Biltmore tower shot in 1930, looking northeast toward DeSoto Fountain and the Venetian Pool.

A view of Pioneer Village looking north along Santa Maria Street toward the Biltmore. The colonial-styled homes were designed by John and Coulton Skinner and John E. Pierson and still stand today, surrounded on both sides by the golf course of the Riviera Country Club, formerly the south eighteen holes of the Biltmore course.

One. Just on the other side of that artery is Henry S. West Lab Elementary School, a public institution so highly regarded that parents register their children at birth, hoping to qualify for kindergarten admission five years hence.

Granada also skirts another campus in this neighborhood, that of the University of Miami, perhaps George Merrick's grandest vision come to pass. It was he who donated the original 160 acres upon which it sits, and Merrick who contributed the original endowment. Although his $5 million pledge was to be matched with $5 million promised by other community leaders, those funds never materialized. Merrick, however, stood good as his word.

The original campus was obliterated by the hurricane of 1926. But despite a rocky beginning (it was more than twenty-five years before the administration building begun in the 1920s was finally completed), grow and prosper it has, becoming a major American university, enrolling some thirteen thousand and standing as an unparalleled source of pride and cultural identity for so many South Florida residents.

From the University, Granada carries on northward, past gracious mansions fronting the golf courses, the sprawling Biltmore Hotel (sometimes it seems all Gables roads lead to the Biltmore), on past Coral Way and the site of the original Merrick grapefruit plantation, where all this started. It ventures past Merrick's boyhood home, and that of fabled Coral Gables land salesman Doc Dammers, about the grounds of Granada Golf Course, the oldest continuously operated nine-hole layout in the United States, and the imposing Coral Gables Country Club, all the way north and west to the intersection of Red Road and Tamiami Trail. There, Country Club Prado forms perhaps the most lovely of the city's storied entrances, brides-to-be are so desiring of having their wedding parties photographed in that spot, they sometimes have to queue.

Riviera and Granada curl past all that and more, and those are enticing paths, to be sure. But history will take us down those routes by and by. Today, the path is slightly more direct, a straight northward shot up Le Jeune, named after a young Belgian who came to the area about the same time as did the Merrick family, and who became a neighbor and fellow citrus grower before selling his land for the development—Le Jeune got a cool million in cash and a note for much more to come, but that is another story.

*J*ust north of the bridge that crosses the Coral Gables Waterway and west of Le Jeune is one of the planned villages to be encountered in Coral Gables today. In this case it is the Dutch South African Village, one of seven that were begun in the early days, with as many more conceived but never brought off the ground.

LEFT: University of Miami students relax between classes. BELOW: The first class of the University's medical school in 1953. While they had no way of knowing, the medical school would go on to become one of the finest academic and research institutions in the country.

Unique Chinese Village, Coral Gables, Florida
182
17800

ABOVE: The Chinese Village, one of the many villages envisioned by Merrick to lend architectural variety to the city, proved so notable as to merit its own postcard.
BELOW: The Antilla Hotel, completed in 1925, was one of the city's earliest, predating the Biltmore by more than a year. Built in the 1100 block of Ponce de Leon Boulevard, it became a popular dining and dancing spot. It was unfortunately demolished before historic preservation ordinances could be written.

In 1926, Merrick, by all accounts, had begun to feel the effects of a cooling Florida real estate market and was casting about for ideas to revitalize interest in his development. In conjunction with a group of Ohio investors, which included a former governor of the state, he launched an ambitious program designed to restore credibility to Florida investment and offer some variety in architecture for prospective home buyers from the north.

As a result, here and there in the Gables, one will also find the Colonial Village (sometimes referred to as Florida Pioneer Village), Chinese Village, Italian Village, French City Village, French Country Village, and, further north along Le Jeune, French Normandy Village. Among those planned but doomed by the collapse of the boom and the ensuing Great Depression were the Spanish Bazaar, Persian Town, Mexican Pioneer and Hacienda Villages, Tangier Villages, and the Neapolitan Baroque Villages. A tantalizing prospect to be sure, imagining those lost dreams made real.

Those that remain, however, are a living testament to Merrick's rare blend of fancy and practicality, of visionary spirit and entrepreneurial

savvy. It may be a startling sight, to be winding down an otherwise unremarkable block of pleasant suburban homes and encounter a walled enclave of Chinese homes with dragon artifacts and blue-tiled roofs, but it also seems good exercise for the soul.

At hypothetical mile marker 6.4 of this day's tour, we have reached that great diagonal artery of Uniform System Highway One, sometimes referred to as America's original Main Street, which runs 2,209 miles up the East Coast, all the way from Key West to Fort Kent, Maine, on the Canadian border. This particular stretch of Main Street opened in 1916 and was named Dixie Highway by legendary Miami developer Carl Fisher. Dixie Highway, America's Main Street, or U.S. Highway Number One it may be, but in the hearts of many Gables planners and residents past and present, it is an asphalt abomination, a scar and a barrier that defies all attempts to ameliorate.

As a six-lane, main commuting artery connecting Miami with the many bedroom communities of South Dade, U.S. 1 carries nearly one hundred thousand vehicles a day through the Gables. In comparison, the eight-lane Dolphin Expressway moves about 145,000 vehicles per day. But the Dolphin has no crosswalks, no intersections, no business entrances and egresses, and of course, no pedestrians traffic to contend with as well. No other surface thoroughfare in Coral Gables, nor in Miami-Dade County—not many in the entire country for that matter—carries the daily volume of traffic that U.S. 1 does. Call this growling, roaring behemoth testimony to the drawing power of South Florida if you will, but know that such is the most pleasant epithet that will likely be hurled its way.

Even in the 1920s, Merrick realized that the highway was a formidable barrier between the northern half of his city and the inviting sea, but at the time Coral Gables was being developed, the adjoining right-of-way of the Florida East Coast Railway was an even greater concern. Always eager to turn a liability into an asset, Merrick had ideas to insulate his populace from the nuisance: several of his promotional brochures promised a lushly

Grove. Merrick offered residents of this tract, which occupied land where University of Miami dormitories now stand, what he considered an unbeatable swap: turn in your old Gables lot, get in return two in the Golden Gate section, adjoining the MacFarlane development (where other Bahamian settlers were building homes) just south of U.S. 1 and east of Le Jeune.

What ultimately swung the deal, however, illustrates the impact this transportation corridor has had on the local populace from the beginning. To get to school, black children of the day had to walk

planted three-hundred-foot wide corridor running the breadth of the city, with inviting fountains and walkways, and anchored by an architectural wonder of a railway station, so that the necessary monster of transport might at least be dealt with in style.

While he might never have conceived of an elevated electrical railway to lift the problem straight off the face of the earth, Merrick surely would have embraced that solution as an agreeable compromise. He knew that Coral Gables could only exist, in its infancy at least, as a commuter-based bedroom community serving nearby Miami, and went to great lengths to assure easy passage by trolley and automobile between the two. But what he might do with today's U.S. 1 is another matter.

The barrier figured historically in another way as well. When Merrick was setting out the original boundaries of Coral Gables, one of the complications he encountered was the existence of a Bahamian immigrant community smack in the middle of his proposed development, an enclave that predated even the black settlement in Coconut

ABOVE: Two friends share a private moment together at the Coral Gables Farmer's Market. RIGHT: The entrance to one of the dozens of historic landmark properties in Coral Gables. Few cities this size in the country have such a high density of protected properties and buildings.

all the way from their Gables settlement to Coconut Grove, crossing the Florida East Coast Railroad right-of-way in the process. According to Florida International University historian Marvin Dunn, parents found the elimination of this deadly threat the most compelling reason of all to make the move. In any case, move they did, and the settlement has remained to this day, along with George Washington Carver Middle School and St. Mary's First Missionary Baptist Church, which dates from 1927.

Present-day residents of Golden Gate one day hope to place the subdivision in the National Register of Historic Places, along with the adjoining MacFarlane Homestead District, where subsidized Arquitectonica-designed bungalows have come to sprout alongside 1920s- and 1930s-styled bungalows and shotgun structures occurring nowhere else in Coral Gables.

The light at the intersection of U.S. 1 and Le Jeune Road changes, and the growling of the traffic beast calms, however momentarily, giving us the

Detail of the Coral Gables Police and Fire Station, a Phineas Paist design, completed in 1939 by the WPA. The two city departments used the building until 1975, when they moved to larger quarters. The building still stands at 285 Aragon. RIGHT: The multi-million-dollar Doris and Phil Sanford Fire Station, serving south Gables, at 11911 Old Cutler Road, completed in 1993. The station is the third and latest addition to a department that enjoys one of only 28 Class I ratings granted nationwide.

opportunity to lunge across those six lanes, cruise through the shadows cast beneath the elevated lines of Metrorail, and emerge unscathed into what is undeniably the motorman's portion of our route.

Just west of the screen of businesses along Le Jeune, the property is primarily residential. To the east, however, extending a quarter-mile to Ponce de Leon Boulevard, and, further north, another quarter-mile to the city's eastward boundary on Douglas Road, lies the strip that contains most of Coral Gables' commercial development. True to Merrick's original vision of craftsmen's quarters and residences being integrated into his ideal commercial district, many bungalows, apartments, and condominiums are to be found scattered throughout the strip. But this is broad-shouldered, no-nonsense Gables territory as well. Merrick had originally planned his commercial area for the northwest section of Coral Gables, close by that lovely Prado entrance and in the path of what he accurately foresaw as the direction of later development in Dade County. But some

things turn out for the best. Likely due to the proximity to existing centers of commerce, including Coconut Grove and the city of Miami, the shops and services located eastward, and there they have remained.

The city maintenance yards are here as well, occupying the site Merrick once envisioned as a broad commercial docking basin connected to his canal system and surrounded by warehouses and rail facilities, a shipping center that would link his city with far-flung ports of call. Today there's a small pond at the center of the yard, not quite the size of the Venetian Pool, and in the place of teak cabin cruisers and two-masted sailing vessels rest a few backhoes and front-end loaders, and white city dump trucks piped in orange and green.

Those mundane conveyances will not rest here long, however. Plans have been announced for an upscale shopping mall of regional proportions—The Village of Merrick Park—to soon commence its rising on this site, a center of commerce that city fathers predict will bring area residents back

(CONTINUED ON PAGE 58)

55

Back to the Future

While it is true that most growth in Coral Gables has been confined to changes within the ten square miles that George Merrick had assembled back in the 1920s, it would not be accurate to portray the city's boundaries as fixed for all time. Residents of neighboring communities and developments in Miami-Dade County, attracted by the quality of life in the Gables, have periodically petitioned for annexation into the city. By 1996, total incorporated land area had grown to 11.9 square miles, and later that year the developments of Deering Bay, Snapper Creek Lakes, Pine Bay Estates, and Hammock Lakes were annexed, bringing the total land area to 13.3 square miles.

The continued migration of major business enterprise to Coral Gables continues as well. AT&T International moved its headquarters from New Jersey in 1993, bringing along sixty employees. Today, that operation has grown to 160 staffers. "Each new-to-market job creates another 2.5 positions within Coral Gables," explains Cathy Swanson, the city's development director. "So the six thousand or so employees who have come to town with the 160 multinationals translates into about twenty thousand jobs for our economy."

In addition to the multinationals, local entities such as Baptist Health Systems and Republic National Bank have moved their corporate headquarters to Coral Gables. Baptist brought with it three hundred employees under its umbrella, and Republic National Bank (with twenty-five branches in Miami-Dade and Broward Counties) moved some 180 employees into a fifteen-story, $30-million-plus office building in Coral Gables.

Efforts by the city's Development Department have assisted in the realization of an agreement for construction of a $275 million mixed-use complex on the 8.3-acre site of the present city maintenance yards east of Le Jeune Road and north of Bird Road. The project, designed by the Rouse Company, developers of Bayside and many other formidable urban centers around the country, will comprise twenty acres in all and will include some 120 residential units, office space, and a four-acre public plaza, along with 730,000 square feet of retail space (roughly half the size of the Dadeland shopping mall). The shopping center will be anchored by Neiman-Marcus and by the first Nordstrom's store to come to Florida.

"We're very excited about the future of Coral Gables," Development Director Swanson says. "But we understand that a large part of our appeal has to do with the stable environment we offer. We will maintain the original conception of Coral Gables even as we tailor it for the twenty-first century. We're just fortunate that what most of our residents want is consistent with what our business leaders want: a great place to live and work."

Republic National Bank is just one of many corporations that has moved its headquarters to Coral Gables. Others include Baptist Health Care Systems of South Florida and AT&T International.

from their Marco Polo-like forays to the newer malls—Dadeland, Cocowalk, Bayside, and The Falls—which have grown up in other parts of Miami-Dade County over the years.

Across the intersection of busy Bird Road, where Coral Gables High School sits, development softens for a mile or so, reverting more to apartments, condominiums, and the occasional office building, including the world headquarters of the International Junior Chamber of Commerce. At this author's imagined mile marker 7.3, the French Normandy Village sits, eleven town homes in this characteristic fifteenth-century style. Though pressed into service in the 1930s as dormitories for men attending the University of Miami, and later as billets for servicemen during World War II, the structures are once again family homes.

The eighteen holes of the Riviera Country Club were carved from the Biltmore Hotel's course. Riviera is now one of the premier clubs in Greater Miami.

Once buffered by a swath of greensward, when Le Jeune still retained its original two-lane George Merrick configuration, the still-attractive homes sit cheek-by-jowl at roadside, as unexpected and diverting a sight in this part of the Gables as a Norman cottage would be in Sevilla: one more thing to keep driving in Coral Gables interesting.

At mythical marker 7.6, the intersection of University Drive and Le Jeune, are the San Sebastian Apartments, originally designed by Coral Gables' supervising architect Phineas Paist as a residence for employees of the Coral Gables Corporation. The San Sebastian opened in 1925, and with seventy apartments and seventy-five hotel rooms was the largest in the city. After the collapse of 1926, the building served as a dormitory and office building for the campus-less University of Miami through the 1930s and 1940s. In fact it remained University property until 1967, when it once again became an apartment building, still exuding its original charm and offering affordable, ready access to the heart of Coral Gables, just as George Merrick had intended. Such options are not inconsequential in a city where even starter homes and fixer-uppers, when they can be found, fetch two hundred thousand dollars and more.

Further north, just short of the intersection of

Coral Way and Le Jeune, the route offers a glimpse of the newly done facade of the Publix Supermarket, tucked away behind its sizable parking lot. It might seem a mundane site to note on our tour, but that's one thing about the Gables: there's always plenty more than meets the eye. With its deep sienna hues and Mediterranean Revival curves trimmed out in cream and green, this most utilitarian of structures nonetheless offers a clue to the determination of modern-day Coral Gables residents to maintain and restore the characteristic architecture of its origins.

Some seventy years ago, George Merrick and supervising architect Phineas Paist, along with designer Denman Fink and landscaper Frank Button, collaborated on a vision derived from many sources—part Mediterranean Revival, part City Beautiful, part pure fancy of the participants. The grand entrances, the plazas, the broad and curving boulevards, the lush plantings, the architectural harmony of public and private buildings that characterize the oldest sections of the city: it is all testament to a rare balance of talent, ambition, vision, and energy. It is even more amazing to realize that the bulk of this legacy, executed few

BELOW: The Coral Gables City Commission gathers for its historic first meeting on February 29, 1928, with Mayor Doc Dammers presiding and George Merrick seated at the head of the table. Former Mayor Fred Hartnett recalled that early proposals were put forward by Merrick and his associates, acting as officers of the Coral Gables Corporation. "Then they'd all stand up, go around to the other side of the table and take their seats as city officials, so they could vote upon what had just been set before them."
RIGHT: City Hall, listed in the National Register of Historic Places, features a striking rotunda patterned after the Philadelphia Mercantile Exchange.

other places in such scope and cohesiveness, was brought into being in the five brief years between 1921 and 1926.

But as Marjory Stoneman Douglas has said, "Sure, we had a boom, and then the boom busted." For a long time following that bust of 1926, nothing much was built in Coral Gables.

In a television interview, longtime Gables resident Tom Thorpe once described the aftermath of the boom and bust in terms appropriate to the long slumber of Sleeping Beauty: avenues flanked by characteristic coral pink sidewalks and socketless street lamps trailed off into rubble at the edge of piney woods. Grand homes sat unfinished or abandoned, open roofs and vacant windows visible behind untended shrubbery.

The original administration building at the University of Miami, devastated by the hurricane of 1926, would remain a steel and concrete skeleton for a quarter of a century. In 1932, a total of four building permits were issued in Coral Gables.

When the city was revitalized in the years following World War II, something of the enthusiasm for the original vision had been lost. Bauhaus and cold modernism had replaced romanticism in architectural thinking. While building codes remained stringent, a new generation was far less zealous about following in historic footsteps and was far more interested in expressing its own reawakened

The majestic Colonnade was originally built as the offfices for the Coral Gables Corporation. Later, it was used as a location for movie sets and as a bank. In 1988, a hotel and office building were added in accordance with a plan by Spillis Candela & Partners.

spirit of optimism and plenty. Characteristic American thinking: a fresh start, and a fresh look.

The result was some three decades of helter-skelter development in the name of progress, in commercial building and residential alike. It doesn't take an architect's eye to follow the course of history in Coral Gables. And such might have continued had not a confluence of factors in the 1970s reawakened community interest in its unique heritage. A revitalized city leadership and historic preservation office set about educating the populace as to the value of its legacy and encouraging restoration and utilization of traditional design elements through special tax and zoning variance incentives. A supermarket facade might seem a matter of insignificance in some ways; but in other ways, it is a symbol and a bellwether, an indication that certain timeless principles may have finally reached "gut" level.

Just north of the market, we encounter what in many ways is the most significant of the many roadways in Coral Gables. Coral Way crosses Le Jeune here. Or rather it once did. Today, one can still turn westward onto that gracious street where in 1898 George Merrick's father came to settle and grow fruits and vegetables. Here, the original Gables Road runs beneath the imposing facade of the City Hall, one of the few important structures to be completed following the bust. A collaboration between Phineas Paist and Harold Steward, the structure was completed in 1928 at a cost of two hundred thousand dollars and still houses the principal functions of city government. Legend has it that area residents were invited to throw mud on the rock walls of the building as it was being completed, in order to give it that aged look. If true, this may constitute the only instance in American history when city officials requested that mud be slung their way.

We could walk the path down the oak-shrouded tunnel of Coral Way, past the Merrick's family house, past the residence of master salesman Doc Dammers, through land that was once nothing but pine barren and grapefruit patch and a burning vision of something to come in a young boy's mind, but we won't, not yet. Today, we're taking the opposite tack at this intersection, heading east on what was once Coral Way but is now known as Miracle Mile.

It's not a mile, of course (it runs for just half that distance over to Douglas Road and the eastern boundary of the city), and as far as its miraculous aspect goes, that is more the creation of public relations executive George K. Zain than any designation born of historical event. Zain and his wife Rebyl envisioned this strip of commercial retail development in 1940 and named it after a string of other such successful shopping stretches about the country. Skeptics are reported to have expressed some doubt about the project: "Sure. It'll be a miracle if anything ever develops here," one wag said. Nonetheless, the idea took hold.

Brought to completion in 1955, the "Mile" has housed its share of legendary entrepreneurs over the years: the F. W. Woolworth Company opened an enormous branch of its five and dime; Elizabeth Arden maintained a popular salon there; the Miracle Theatre attracted moviegoers for nearly forty years and lives on today as the home of a professional theatre.

The Biscayne Miracle Mile Cafeteria has been a staple of its namesake street since 1946. "Nothing fancy," says one longtime patron. "Just great food, wonderful servers, and low prices."

Today, the broad sidewalks flanking the Mile still bustle: upscale clothiers, antique shops, beauty salons, travel agents. The Biscayne Cafeteria, a favorite since its establishment in 1946, operates today under the ownership of Alex Nunez, a Miami native who remembers first coming to the restaurant at the age of two. One of the original Mile merchants, hairstyling legend J. Baldi, still plies his trade there, although the shop is now owned by Judi Ashworth. (You'll also find Baldi mentioned in *Ripley's Believe It Or Not,* given the anomaly of his work with his name.) A French restaurant, Le Provencal, anchors one end of the Mile, a Denny's the other, a Starbucks Coffee emporium in between. A Barnes & Noble superstore has taken over the old Woolworth site, testimony to the rising profile of Coral Gables as a true "book" city.

Fifteen years ago, no literary publicist ever included Coral Gables on the itinerary of a best-selling author's promotional tour. Then Mitchell Kaplan and his uncle Julius Ser opened Books & Books (at the time, the city's only full-service bookstore), on the corner of Aragon and Salzedo, just north of the Mile. And everything literary began to change.

Kaplan and Ser not only sold books, they became purveyors of reading and the literary impulse in Coral Gables and Miami as well. Kaplan soon began to envision a community celebration of the book, with author appearances and readings, cookbook demonstrations, a week or more of seminars and discussions, children's storytelling,

antiquarian exhibits and more, the enterprise spilling outdoors, under tents and building overhangs, requiring that the very streets of the city be cordoned off as a hundred thousand or more citizens thronged to participate.

"Come back to earth, Mitchell," one skeptic was heard to murmur. But the Miami Book Fair, the largest community festival of books and reading in the U.S., has indeed come to be. Rare is the author who, these days, does not demand that the promotional tour include Miami and Coral Gables on the itinerary.

One other establishment to be noted before we leave the Mile is the Colonnade Building, the original headquarters and sales center for George Merrick's Coral Gables Corporation. The building is another Phineas Paist design (along with Walter DeGarmo and Paul Chalfin) and was completed in 1926 at a cost of six hundred thousand dollars. While the original structure is dwarfed by the modern office tower and hotel that connects and rises just to the north, its meticulously rendered facade and elegant, rotunda-capped interior remain intact, a monument to Merrick's trademark style and sense of elegance. If this was the

sales office, prospects must have murmured, just imagine what the city itself will become.

The last leg of our route veers northward here, up Ponce de Leon Boulevard for the final mile and a half. It is a portion of our trail that burrows into the deepest veins of Coral Gables history and leads toward the face of the future as well.

As even those unfamiliar with Coral Gables history might guess, the Boulevard is named after the Spanish explorer, though history suggests that he never came ashore in these parts during his search for the Fountain of Youth. Ponce did discover Florida, however, and in a roundabout way it might be argued that he made Coral Gables possible after some 408 years. Undoubtedly, he was the first and quintessential dreamer to come to these shores, and in that regard, George Merrick certainly was following this captain's lead.

Just north of Miracle Mile is the intersection of Alhambra Circle, which crosses Le Jeune after running down from one of the four grand entrances Merrick had executed for his city. The idea of these entrances (Merrick had planned

Enjoying a walk outdoors, these workers stroll in the shadow of the massive columns of the Colonnade Building on Miracle Mile. The original building was completed in 1926 to house the sales offices of George Merrick's Coral Gables Corporation. LEFT: Mitchell Kaplan, proprietor of Books & Books and architect of the Miami Book Fair, the largest literary festival in the U.S., ensconced amidst the stacks of his shop. The bookstore is located within the historic John M. Stabile Building, at the corner of Aragon Avenue and Salzedo Street. The shop originally functioned as an earthen-floor establishment for the purveying of ornamental building blocks.

The pleasant climate of the region has afforded residents of Coral Gables any number of outdoor diversions, none of them more remarkable than this open-air bowling center which once operated in the city. Ten-pin activities were also briefly a feature of the old Coliseum at 1500 Douglas Road. The latter structure seemed doomed as a cultural venue almost from the day it was built, and was razed in 1993 to make way for commercial development.

eight in all) was to announce the concept of Coral Gables to the visitor immediately and mark the abandonment of the ordinary world in a very clear fashion.

The Commercial Entrance, at Alhambra and Douglas Road, designed by Denman Fink and the second to be completed (in 1923), is in many ways the simplest and perhaps most organically proportioned of the lot. While some six hundred feet long, the structure is built lower to the ground than its awe-inspiring cousins, more in keeping with the surrounding landscape. Like the others, it makes extensive use of the native oolitic limestone sometimes referred to as coral rock, though in this case the texture is more rough-

hewn (Merrick's own brother Charles was the stone mason for the project). The central arch through which traffic was to be routed toward the business section of the city is Romanesque, spacious but simply adorned, not nearly so grand as that of Granada or Douglas. The aspect created is of approaching some walled city of antiquity, of graciousness more than pretense, of welcome for the weary traveler, and promise for those in search.

Further along Ponce, as it is referred to locally, we pass the Coral Gables Elementary School, at the corner of Minorca Avenue. The school, designed in the ubiquitous Mediterranean Revival style and constructed in three stages between 1923 and 1926, was the first public school built in Coral Gables and is still in use today.

While some modern architects have questioned the use of the Mediterranean style for the tropical climate, touting the broad overhangs and wraparound porches of the Florida cracker style instead,

TOP: An early Miracle Mile postcard. RIGHT: A more modern view of Miracle Mile is chock full of shops and restaurants. BELOW: The Granada Entrance (at Tamiami Trail), as it appeared shortly after its completion in 1922. Designed by Denman Fink, it is said to have been modeled after the entrance gate to its namesake city in Spain.

this building is unquestionably a marriage of form and function, arranged about two central open courtyards, its arcaded loggias providing shade from the tropical sun and natural channels for the prevailing breezes to course. Walking these pleasant cloisters on a hot summer day while the coastal winds glide and the summer-schoolers chant their muffled lessons somewhere in the ever-distance gives renewed vitality to Merrick's lofty advertising copy of yesteryear:

"Primary and secondary schools furnish in every city the keenest opportunity for insight as to the make-up of that city's population and the state of its growth or otherwise....The Coral Gables Grammar School building, now almost completed, marks another advance—better homes, larger breathing spaces in lawns and parks, better air and water, and a far better influence

through beautiful things which inspire high ideals in the minds of children."

Another half-mile northward now, on past the point where a glance to the east in the once-upon-a-time would have yielded a glimpse of the Coral Gables Coliseum above the other rooftops fronting Douglas Road. That seventy-five-hundred-seat auditorium, completed in 1927, booked Will Rogers and a rodeo as its opening act, but its fortunes rapidly declined, along with the collapse of the local and national economies. A white ele-

ABOVE and RIGHT: Assembly and Maypole activities from the early days of Coral Gables Elementary School, 105 Minorca Avenue. Architect Richard Kiehnel designed the building in a Mediterranean Revival style. It was constructed from 1923–26. FAR RIGHT: Coral Gables Elementary School today still retains its original architectural flavor.

phant essentially from the day the doors opened, the coliseum went through various incarnations—ice skating rink, bowling alley, training center for World War II servicemen, health club—before it was demolished in the 1990s to make way for an office supply mega-store.

In a short while we pass the Coral Gables Woman's Club, constructed in 1937 by the Works Progress Administration. It is also the second site of the Coral Gables Library, which began its life in clubrooms of the Douglas Entrance building, space donated by who else but George Merrick. Merrick's wife, Eunice Peacock, she of the pioneer-

ing Coconut Grove Peacocks, was one of the founders of the Woman's Club and the garden club, and the general overseer of staff operations behind the scenes of Merrick's operations. She had seen Coconut Grove, Miami, and Miami Beach grow out of territory so wild that once a ship's captain offered to take his passengers back to New England at his own expense rather than see them disembark upon such frightful-looking shores. Why then should she have doubted her new husband's dream, however grandly stated: "...to reclaim the wilderness and make it bloom, to build schools and playgrounds, universities and churches, to put sunshine and air within the reach of families born and reared in smoky tenement towns. A fine thing, indeed, to build houses rich and full of pleasantries and to people them with men and women eager to live brighter, healthier and more useful lives. There is a savor of omnipotence about it."

At the intersection of Ponce and Antilla, where the Woman's Club sits, the fingerling road of East Ponce de Leon sprouts off to the northeast, where it once coursed through the grandest entrance of

(CONTINUED ON PAGE 77)

Beyond Mediterranean—The Village Concept

It was George Merrick's original plan to build many of the homes in Coral Gables out of the native coral rock, the easily quarried and shaped porous limestone foundation that constitutes, literally, the bedrock of South Florida. This coquina, or oolite, as it is also known, was used in the construction of the Merrick family home and several other of the earliest Gables houses. With soaring demand, it soon became evident that the all-coral concept was impractical. In fact, the use of concrete and block likely allowed for a greater range of expression within Mediterranean design than might have otherwise developed.

The village concept came about in like serendipitous manner, a new direction in home styling undertaken in 1925, as Merrick came to understand the need to appeal to the broadest possible range of buying tastes and the advantages of involving others in the capital-intensive process of development. Thus began the joint venture between Merrick, the American Building Corporation, and

former Ohio Governor Myers Cooper. It was a $75 million project that was touted at the time as the largest home-development project in history.

"Seven Miami and five New York architects are uniting in working out the details of the great planning of house construction," Merrick proclaimed in one of his many promotional booklets. "Thirteen styles are being used, drawn from various regions and nations which harmonize with the Mediterranean style now in use."

Fewer than eighty of the one thousand homes planned were built, and of those fourteen villages Merrick conceived, only seven ever took on worldly shape. The vestiges we have, however, are enduring proof of the power of this dreamer's fancy: Florida Pioneer Village (sometimes more appropriately called Southern Colonial), bordering the Riviera Country Club golf course on Santa Maria Street, designed by J. L. and Coulton Skinner, of Miami; French 18th Century (or French City), in the 1000 Block of Hardee Road, by Mott Schmidt and Phillip Goodwin of New York City; French Normandy Village, at Le Jeune and Viscaya, also by the Skinner team; French Country, in the 500 Block of Hardee, by E. A. Albright of Miami, Goodwin, and Frank Forster of New York; Dutch South African, on Le Jeune at Maya Avenue, by Marian Wyeth of New York; the Italian Village, a sprawling area just south of Bird Road, between Granada Boulevard and Riviera Drive, where Miamian Robert Weed was the architect.

LEFT: Perhaps the most arresting of them all is the eight-unit Chinese Village ensconced behind an elegantly ported and gated wall on Riviera Drive just south of U.S. 1. Henry Killam Murphy designed this grouping of homes after a traditional Chinese compound; the bright glazed tile roofs, statuary, and other traditional decorative touches make the village a near hallucinatory experience for the unprepared visitor. BELOW: The French City Village was also one of the more popular of Merrick's village communities.

The modern glass of Ponce de Leon Plaza reflects the historical looking tower of Commercebank. The image can be seen at the intersection of Ponce de Leon Boulevard and Alhambra Circle. RIGHT: This plaque commemorates the incorporation of Coral Gables on April 29, 1925. It was commissioned by the local chapter of the Daughters of the American Revolution in 1937.

them all, at the corner of Tamiami Trail, or SW 8th Street, and its namesake road. The Douglas Entrance was designed by Phineas Paist and Walter DeGarmo and took from 1925 to 1927 to complete. At a cost of $1 million, it incorporated a ninety-foot clock tower, apartments, art galleries and retail spaces, as well as a lavish ballroom and club suites in buildings flanking its archway. Surrounding development was to cover some ten acres and suggest the makeup of a typical Mediterranean village square. In fact, the original name of the entrance was La Puerta del Sol (The Gate of the Sun) after the central square of Madrid. The name was later changed to honor John and Mary Douglas, fellow Dade County homesteaders who also maintained a grapefruit plantation on part of the city's original acreage.

Despite its imposing nature, the Douglas Entrance was actually scheduled for demolition in the late 1960s before a coalition of preservationists and a local architectural firm joined forces to save it. While completely renovated and surrounded by office and retail structures, and while traffic no longer runs through the square, the entrance itself remains much as it originally was, its other-era grandeur still intact.

Across SW 8th Street/Tamiami Trail, Ponce de Leon curls through the northernmost corner of the city, a Balkanesque thumb of land surrounded by the ever-westward sprawl from Miami and Little Havana. Like some narrow corridor cut to allow access to a distant sea, Coral Gables does manage a brush with Flagler Street here, 10.3 miles from our journey's point of origin.

There's a modest coral rock pylon with an oft-disappearing wooden sign that announces entry to Merrick's city here, and along these brief blocks Ponce de Leon adopts a curvaceousness that is characteristic of the City Beautiful ideal. There's an insurance agency ensconced in a typical Mediterranean revival bungalow nearby, the sort that Merrick promoted as a necessary complement to the grander homes elsewhere. (Merrick once wrote, "There is nothing in Coral Gables' restrictions which will prevent the building of a modest home, providing it is of masonry. There are streets in large numbers where cost restrictions are as low as $4,000. But the man who desires a $10,000 or

$25,000 home will naturally select a street where restrictions are higher.")

Just down the street is Wesley United Methodist Church, representing one of the "eight major congregations" Merrick was fond of mentioning in his literature. ("Spiritually as well as in a cultural sense, Coral Gables has progressed at a pace which is in no sense behind her material advancement.") The street names chiseled into the idiosyncratic stone markers here—Boabadilla, Carmona, Fonseca, Marabella—derive in the Gables from Merrick's fascination with *Tales of the Alhambra,* and they ring equally with their inherent poetry.

In its modest aspect there is also something of the feel of the outpost here on the northern border of the city. The tangled sawgrass and mangroves in the south form a kind of primeval starting point, a reminder of where all Florida progress began. The route northward offers a look at the diverse shapes and richness of that development. Here, gazing across Flagler Street at the mercados and the ferreterias and the lavadoras that march out from Little Havana to line its northern verge, we have a glimpse of the landscape of the future.

"*In history and tradition,* climate and foliage, Florida is more closely allied with Spain than with any other country," Merrick once proclaimed. Ironic, perhaps, that his often-idealized renderings of themes Hispanic should have come to blend with a very real influx of these same cultures, but somehow it seems appropriate, and, on this warm summer's day, pleasing as well.

The La Palma Hotel, a mainstay of Coral Gables since the 1920s, is today an office building and a restaurant with an elegant shaded courtyard. It is a favorite gathering spot for the lunchtime crowd.

PART TWO

The Merrick Years

W HEN ASKED FOR her opinion of the founder of Coral Gables, legendary historian and novelist Marjory Stoneman Douglas replied, "George Merrick was a man with a great deal of foresight." It was a terse evaluation, something the casual observer might have attributed to the speaker's advancing age. After all, she was 101 at the time Ellen Uguccioni, the city's director of historic preservation, spoke with her. But elsewhere during this televised interview for the city-produced program "The Good Ole Days," Ms. Douglas displayed a great clarity of memory, suggesting other interpretations for her grudging assessment.

"Merrick hired me to write a booklet on Coral Gables," she said later, referring to a 1920s' promotional pamphlet entitled *Coral Gables: Miami Riviera, A Great American City Region*. "He paid me three hundred dollars for it and he used it a lot. Later, he hired Rex Beach [then a popular writer of adventure novels] to write one. He paid Beach twenty thousand dollars and hardly used it at all." (The sum paid Beach has been reported elsewhere at eighteen thousand dollars, but one grasps Ms. Douglas's point.)

Though long an opponent of thoughtless development (her father was sounding warnings about Everglades depletion as early as 1910), Ms. Douglas found much to applaud in her 1925 treatment of Merrick's project. Granted, her publication was not nearly as florid as Rex Beach's assessment, which was entitled *The Miracle of Coral Gables* and contained such paeans to Merrick as: "His dream was to build a City Beautiful, without blot or blemish, without ugliness or dirt; a city of majestic size but of perfect harmony. A city planned with reverence and with care and built after the old Grecian ideal

LEFT: In 1927, the First National Bank was headquartered in this building on Ponce de Leon Boulevard. Now it is home to a popular cafe. RIGHT: Entitled *The Miracle of Coral Gables*, this publication was written by Rex Beach, and touted Merrick's dream to build a city "without blot or blemish, without ugliness or dirt . . . of perfect harmony."

Solomon and Althea Merrick at their parsonage home in Duxbury, Massachusetts, where Rev. Merrick was pastor of the Old Pilgrim Congregational Church. The photo was taken in 1898, shortly before Solomon and his son, George, then twelve (and seen holding his bicycle) left to begin life in their new home near Miami.

that nothing is so sacred as the beautiful: that was his vision."

Nonetheless, Ms. Douglas's pamphlet praised Merrick for his comprehensive planning and intentions to wed his vision to the essence of the place upon which it was being built: "That is why Coral Gables is so remarkable. It is a city, not at all politically so, but a city in such intimate relation with the region in which it is built that it is more like a great garden set with houses, a park where all the people can live to their best capacities than a city in the old sense."

Nor did the still-salty lady find any detractions worth mentioning on the day of the television interview, some sixty-six years later. In fact, were she pressed on the matter, she might have been willing to concede what the most cursory examination of history suggests: George Merrick was a rare amalgam of visionary and pragmatist. He was at once a poet and a businessman, a lover of nature and a developer, a utopian and a politician. And the proof is to be found in the legacy he left behind: the city of Coral Gables, Florida.

George Merrick came to South Florida in 1898, a twelve-year-old boy accompanying his father Solomon, a Congregationalist minister from Massachusetts, in search of more hospitable living conditions for his family. The Merricks had lost a daughter, Ruth (one of seven Merrick children), to pneumonia, and Solomon Merrick's health was beginning to decline as well. As George Merrick once described the situation (in a letter included in Katheryne Ashley's 1985 biography, *George E. Merrick and Coral Gables, Florida*):

"The old New England street in front of the Colonial parsonage was a snow canyon, the banks towering so high that Dr. Noyes, traveling horseback to his score of pneumonia patients, standing in the stirrups, could not reach their tops....There had been over forty pneumonia deaths in the old Cape Cod village within the week, and as many more lay at death's door nearby our parsonage home, where death, too, had just visited....So terrible was the blizzard that it was impossible to bury all the fast accumulating victims. The painful New England Quinsy, the chronic type of rheumatism, was rendering life unbearable for my mother and father. One evening, during that terrible time, there came to the parsonage an old friend of my minister father's who had just returned from Florida, with veritable Marco Polo tales of a wonderful new fairy land of enchantment around a newly planted town on Biscayne Bay. No greater contrast could be imagined than that between those tales of enchanted sunshine in the South and the frigid scene of ice, desolation and death all around Cape Cod."

The elder Merrick needed to hear no more. Upon learning that a tract of farm-

land might be available at a reasonable price, Solomon Merrick set off for South Florida with his young son George in tow. Though a yellow fever outbreak had placed Miami (then a garrison for troops engaged in the Spanish-American War) in quarantine, Solomon Merrick was unfazed. He and George spent several months with a colleague near Jupiter, waiting out the siege, then traveled on to the pine barrens southwest of the fledgling settlement of Miami, where they took possession of the 160-acre William Gregory homestead: purchase price, eleven hundred dollars.

The property contained little: a one-room cabin and one-half acre planted in guava trees. Yet Solomon Merrick had found his home. He used what money he had left for a wagon, a mule, and supplies, and brought the rest of the family to Florida. Perhaps in return for his faith, the meager guava plantation bore heavily that year and the family realized

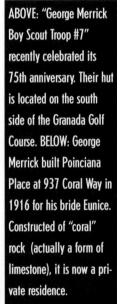

ABOVE: "George Merrick Boy Scout Troop #7" recently celebrated its 75th anniversary. Their hut is located on the south side of the Granada Golf Course. BELOW: George Merrick built Poinciana Place at 937 Coral Way in 1916 for his bride Eunice. Constructed of "coral" rock (actually a form of limestone), it is now a private residence.

grance of blossoms in the air, all combined to fire that first image in a young boy's mind of what might arise one day from that rich and mysterious wilderness.

The collection of poetry that Merrick would one day publish, *Songs of the Wind on a Southern Shore* (1920), is in fact composed largely of tributes to the beauty of the landscape that enveloped him, and provides us with hints of just what visions he was capable of. As his poem "The Cloud Mountains of Florida" attests:

something in excess of two hundred dollars for their crop, enough to ensure their survival. They called their plantation "Guavonia," naturally enough, and planted vegetables, avocado (which Merrick referred to as "alligator pears"), orange and grapefruit trees, and were able to add to the size of the board and batten frame house.

G*eorge Merrick's mother,* Althea, who had been a college art teacher (her young brother Denman Fink was to become a well-known artist and would figure large in the Merrick future) determined to organize a school on the premises, where George continued his education, along with his brothers and sisters and other children from the area. As the oldest child, it fell to George to drive the family wagon into the distant city of Miami to sell the family produce and trade for the necessary supplies. Letters that he wrote describing those solitary, four-hour journeys through the largely uninhabited woodlands suggest that he had plenty of opportunity to wonder and dream: "In those days no one else would pass in a whole night on that road, and sometimes not for days . . . ."

Perhaps it was one evening on the way back to Guavonia, when the angle of moonlight and the ghostly shapes of the clouds, the tropical breezes and the swaying shadows of the pines, the seductive motion of the wagon and the teasing fra-

TOP and RIGHT: George Merrick's elegant boyhood home, now a must on any historic tour of Coral Gables. ABOVE: Solomon Merrick, George's father, upon graduation from Yale Divinity School; Althea Merrick, around 1935, in the living room of her house.

To the south lie the magnificent mountains,
That half-circling the horizon rise;
The mystical, magical, faraway mountains;—
In the depth of the tropical skies.

Nor should it seem unreasonable that dreams of earthly possibility might take shape in young George's mind, for the Merricks' new home was to prove beneficent to the family. They had journeyed to Florida with five children under keep and a sixth was soon to come (youngest brother Richard was one of the first children to be born in the area, in 1903). Obtaining clothing, shoes, even proper food, were considerable difficulties at first, and Solomon Merrick's familiar reassurance— "When the groves begin to bear . . . "—was to become something of a family anthem. In fact, one of the more affecting poems in Merrick's collection contained these lines:

In the days when all was labor
From the morn past evening's sun:
Nor the time to even "neighbor,"
Not an hour for any fun; —

85

"But we will"—my father's saying:—
"When the groves begin to bear!"
Oh that brave and hopeful saying!
And that kept our hearts alive...

As fortune would have it, the groves did begin to bear, and by 1903, the tiny frame house had been transformed into a substantial home constructed in large part of the native oolitic limestone. While not true coral at all, the rock (which is relatively soft when quarried and hardens with exposure to the light and air) nonetheless resembles the saltwater formation, and such a namesake certainly rings with greater poetry. The family, it is said, spent some effort in coming up with a name for the new abode, and one can only imagine the general consternation if the name they had finally agreed upon had been "Oolitic Gables."

Coral Gables it was to be, however, after the rock and the house's many-gabled roof. The structure still stands today at 907 Coral Way. (The house was to later serve as a boarding facility

LEFT: A shot of George Merrick in 1925, at the height of Gables development. Those close to him say he remained undaunted by the reversals that led to the collapse of the original Coral Gables Corporation in the late 1920s—he remained involved in real estate until the very end of his career.
BELOW: Coral Gables As It Was: A view that suggests the power of George Merrick's ability to envision paradise where only groves and piney woods had been.

known as "Merrick Manor" and was to leave family hands for a brief period. It has since been deeded to the city and is now known officially as "Coral Gables Merrick House," serving as a repository of family and city history and open to the public for tours.)

With the family fortunes on the rise, Solomon Merrick encouraged George's passion for learning, enrolling him in Rollins College in Winter Park in 1907, where he was to meet novelist Rex Beach, a Rollins alum. He and Merrick had a number of friends in common, including Merrick's uncle, Denman Fink, who illustrated Beach's novel *The Barriers* while Merrick was still enrolled at Rollins. Beach would go on to publish several more books, and when the time came Merrick was to use Beach's talents and notoriety in the promotion of Coral Gables.

It was Solomon Merrick's intention that his son become an attorney, and George Merrick did in fact enter New York Law School (then a part of Columbia University) in 1908, living at the home of Fink, who was only six years older.

Men of Vision: (From left) Charles Flynn, the first manager of the Biltmore Hotel; George Merrick; John McEntee Bowman, president of the Biltmore Hotel Corporation; and an unidentified colleague at the site of the proposed Tahiti Beach. Merrick envisioned a European-styled Casino and another Biltmore Hotel on these grounds, but it would never be. Today, the exclusive subdivision of Cocoplum occupies the property.

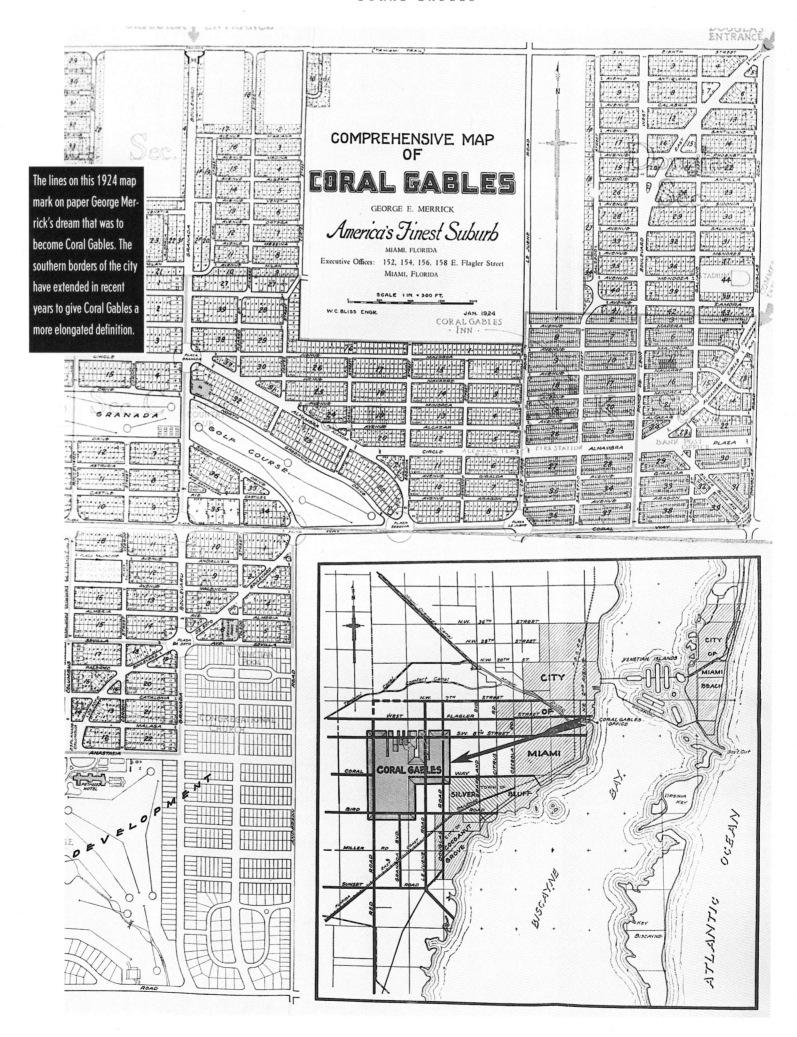

The lines on this 1924 map mark on paper George Merrick's dream that was to become Coral Gables. The southern borders of the city have extended in recent years to give Coral Gables a more elongated definition.

COMPREHENSIVE MAP
OF
CORAL GABLES

GEORGE E. MERRICK

America's Finest Suburb

MIAMI, FLORIDA

Executive Offices: 152, 154, 156, 158 E. Flagler Street
MIAMI, FLORIDA

SCALE 1 IN. = 300 FT.

W.C. BLISS ENGR.   JAN. 1924

While George was never an enthusiastic student of the law—he was writing short stories at the time, one of which won a contest sponsored by the *New York Evening Telegram*—it is quite possible that he would have carried out his father's wishes to become a lawyer out of his fabled love and devotion to the man. As another Merrick letter quoted by Kathryne Ashley goes: "After everyone else was asleep, my father was still up and planning and working for the planting here in this new and wonderful country, seeds, bulbs, and plants. I was inspired by his courage in hardship; his fortitude and perseverance in the sowing and caring for material, spiritual, and intellectual plantings."

The question will never be answered, however. In 1909, Solomon Merrick fell seriously ill, and George dropped out of law school to come home and manage the plantation in the name of a newly formed company, S. G. Merrick and Son. Solomon Merrick died in 1911, but by that time, George had developed an affinity for the endeavors begun by his father, motivated in part, it would seem, to pay homage to his father's dreams. Again, from "When the Groves Begin to Bear":

And the pang to know that after
All these hopes—so long deferred:—

When came chance for joy and laughter:—
He never shared the boons conferred.
He was not here to prove his saying:—
—When the groves began to bear.

Whatever his motivation, George Merrick had by 1918 created one of the most prosperous citrus and agricultural operations in South Florida and had expanded the original 160-acre homestead to some 1,200 acres. He had met and married Eunice Isabella Peacock, of the pioneering Coconut Grove family, in 1916, and along the way had also formed a successful real estate business.

> Eunice Peacock Merrick's family was among the first settlers of Coconut Grove, Florida, where they ran the Peacock Inn. She was born in 1895, married George Merrick in 1916, and lived in Coral Gables until her death in 1989. She was a founder of the Coral Gables Garden Club in 1924 and is credited with naming many of the city's streets.

Perhaps most significantly for modern-day residents of South Florida, Merrick had also begun the process of bringing his most ambitious dreams to fruition. As an article of the day in the *Miami Herald* reported: "The [Merrick] plantation is gradually coming into demand for residence locations. Indeed, the plan is ultimately to incorporate the entire plantation, as the 'Village of Coral Gables' . . . . "

It was not a dream that materialized out of thin air, of course. Solomon Merrick had himself expressed intentions of subdividing a portion of his plantation into five-acre tracts for resale to other retired ministers and professionals, and George Merrick had been involved in real estate development for a number of years. He had become a Dade County commissioner and had participated in the subdivision of several communities, including Goulds and Riverside Heights.

However, his heart had always been set upon accomplishing something special, and that was the creation of an entire planned city, embodying the most gracious and enlightened principles of the time: "A city," in Merrick's own words, "of distinction, character and beauty, which compels the admiration of everyone who sees it." Elsewhere, Merrick referred to the building of Coral Gables as "a wonderful monument to . . . the creation of beauty and the bringing true of dreams." Later, revealing the pragmatic aspect of self that undoubtedly allowed these dreams to take worldly form, he was to add: "Beauty can be made to pay."

Elements that especially attracted Merrick to the development of Coral Gables included the prospect of a blank canvas upon which to work and the absolute authority to proceed as he pleased. Aerial photos of the day show that the original Coral Gables Plantation was, in fact, little more than a vast pine barren, interrupted here and there by groves, or an occasional outbuilding. Furthermore, Merrick was sole owner of the twelve hundred acres that would constitute the core of

his city. By liquidating most of his other real estate holdings, he provided himself with five hundred thousand dollars in cash, and was ready to begin.

It is at this point, the point at which countless other dreamers and schemers have doomed themselves over history, that Merrick made certain decisions that would prove crucial to the success of his plan, and would distinguish him not only as a man of vision but also as a man of wisdom. To put it simply, he had the good sense to sur-

LEFT: Will S. Hammon and son Harley. "Major" Hammon presided over the six-hundred-person tent city which housed laborers during the early days of Coral Gables construction.
ABOVE: A view of "Tent City" worker lodging employed during the early days of Coral Gables.

round himself with a team of experts, men whose varied talents and great ambition were very nearly the equal of his own. "My uncle always had the last say, mind you," said his nephew Donald Kuhn, the son of Merrick's sister Helen, during a recent interview. "But he brought in the very best people there were."

"The very best people" included as chief designer his uncle Denman Fink, a member of the National Academy of Art, a regular illustrator for *Harper's, Heart,* and *Scribner's* magazines; Frank M. Button, landscape architect and assistant engineer for the World's Colombian Exposition of 1893 and designer of Lincoln Park near Chicago (it is reported that Merrick hired him to lay out his twelve hundred acres for a fee of one dollar per acre); and as Chief Architect, Phineas E. Paist, who had studied at Drexel and later in Paris, and who had worked as associate architect on James Deering's estate, Villa Vizcaya. All three, as Merrick himself, had been greatly influenced by the "City Beautiful" movement, introduced to the American

public by exhibits at the World's Colombian Exposition of 1893 in Chicago (and, ironically, about to die out by the time of Coral Gables' founding).

Chief precepts of this movement in city planning were the avoidance of the grid pattern in laying out city streets: the encouragement of broad, winding boulevards; lushly planted medians; and the incorporation of public plazas and fountains to foster a sense of spaciousness and an appreciation of the aesthetic and the naturally beautiful within the course of everyday life.

While the concept of the "planned city" in America dated back to the design of Washington, D.C., the sheer size and diversity of that city masks the intent of its designers for most. Merrick and his advisers were more attuned to the possibilities of such latter-day, more manageable communities bearing the marks of the movement, such as Forest Hills, Mariemont, Shaker Heights, and New Haven. While street design, landscaping, and public amenities obviously derived from "City Beautiful" theory and practices, the choice of the

This is the third house occupied by George Merrick in Coral Gables—designed by H. George Fink, Merrick's cousin, and completed in 1924. It was intended as the showpiece of the new development. The house, with its intricate perimeter wall, still stands at 832 South Greenway Drive.

M3825

signature architectural style was by all accounts that of Merrick himself.

*T*he *Mediterranean Revival Style is,* like that other characteristic South Florida trope, Art Deco, less a true style than a mode of embellishment. Merrick and his wife Eunice had traveled through Central America and Mexico, and it is said that both were devotees of the exotic writings of Washington Irving, especially the Spanish romance *Tales of the Alhambra.* For them, as for most Americans, the maintenance of strict architectural distinctions between the Venetian, the Roman, and the Moorish were of far less importance than the importation of the sense of romance and invigoration to be found not only in Spanish names, but in such tangible aspects as the rich earth-tones and rough textures of the plaster finishes, the colorful barrel-tiled roofs of terra cotta, the exotic flourish of archways, canvas awnings, exposed timbers, wrought iron embellishments, and columned, covered walkways. It is not uncommon to discover design elements of the adobe hacienda and the Venetian palazzo within the same Coral Gables structure, nor, after a bit of familiarity with such eclecticism, does it seem at odds with the pragmatic American spirit so much alive in the 1920s.

Merrick was fond of justifying his choice of styles, often referring to it as the perfect choice for the city's tropical climate. In *Coral Gables: Miami Riviera, Forty Miles of Waterfront,* he reasserted his contention that Florida and Spain were closely connected through everything from history and tradition to climate and foliage.

In his introduction to *Coral Gables: An American Garden City,* French architect Maurice Culot dismisses any theoretical or practical basis for the use of the Mediterranean Revival in Coral Gables. As a practical matter, the use of the so-called Cracker vernacular, with its emphasis on shady overhangs and cross ventilation, would have been a more likely choice. But the fact was that the Mediterranean was a mode associated with the buildings and artifacts of the wealthy, as seen in the paintings of such *fin de siecle* realists as William Poynter and Maxfield Parrish, and in such structures as William Randolph Hearst's castle at San Simeon, Deering's Villa Vizcaya, Mizner's mansions in Palm Beach, et al.

"This was simply the style that he [Merrick] liked," concludes Culot, and he is probably right.

The fortunate thing is that so many who came after Merrick came to appreciate that taste, for surely it is the "look" of Coral Gables that is its most obvious defining characteristic, and its strongest link with its past. The Mediterranean Revival style may be as elusive to define as jazz; but, like jazz, there is no mistaking it when encountered. Those encounters are nowhere more frequent, more varied, or more interesting than in Coral Gables.

Merrick countenanced other styles, clearly: Coral Gables Merrick House and others had been constructed of native rock, incorporating features typical of the New England bungalow, with ample porches and overhangs borrowed from the native Cracker style and employed to capture prevailing breezes and combat the brutal sun. Furthermore, the introduction of the villages concept suggested that even if Merrick was not eclectic in his own tastes, he was wise enough to appeal to a range in others.

Without question, however, he was concerned with maintaining the quality of his vision. As he wrote in a part of *Miami Riviera*: "Every section of the suburb has building restrictions which protect home-owners in every way . . . . All houses are to be of coral rock or stucco [to] insure a high standard

(CONTINUED ON PAGE 100)

Forty Miles of Waterfront, Honest!

In a promotional booklet dated November 15, 1926, and titled **Coral Gables Today**, George Merrick marshalled a wide array of statistics to paint a picture of a city where "development is unremitting." By his account, more than $125 million had been spent on public works, building entrances, plazas, roads, public buildings, and utilities in the five years of the city's existence (and not a dollar in profit taken out, he maintained). There were eighty-six miles of paved streets and ninety miles of sidewalks in place, and contracts had just been let for fifty-one more miles of streets and another two hundred or so miles of sidewalks.

"You have to be careful, though, of how you interpret street-mile counts," offers present-day Public Works Director Al Linero. "It's common practice in the street engineering business to measure both ways of a two-lane road." It is a caution that caused skeptics of yesteryear to question Merrick's often-quoted claim that Coral Gables contained "forty miles of waterfront," an insistence born of the understanding that a Florida development without access to the sea was at a distinct competitive disadvantage.

Merrick went to some pains to prove the truth of his claims:

"Coral Gables has Gulf Stream and ocean frontage extending from Bear Cut, at the northern end of Key Biscayne, to the northern end of Sand Key, a distance of fifteen miles and including Key Biscayne, Soldier Key and Ragged Keys. Key Biscayne, within the city of Coral Gables [at that time], has three miles of ocean frontage and three miles of bay frontage. Along the mainland Coral Gables has over five miles of actual Biscayne Bay frontage and it will have, when completed, over forty miles of actual lot frontage on its inland waterway system."

So, with five miles of actual coastline on Biscayne Bay, six miles constituting the circumference of Key Biscayne, and throwing in another four, presumably garnered from the circumnavigation of the other tiny keys in Merrick's inventory, we derive the figure of fifteen. Public Works Director Linero confirms that there exist today twelve miles of canals in the city, all of them dredged by Merrick, according to plan. Grand total: twenty-seven, a tad shy of forty, without a doubt.

But let's say, for the sake of argument, that Linero is half a mile short in his canal measuring and that, by the time we've reached the very tip-end of the Gables Waterway,

somewhere in the shadow of the Biltmore's tower, we've stretched the count to twenty-seven and one-half miles. That way, we can simply turn about, sail back down the waterway for another twelve and one-half miles, and that is forty miles total in anyone's book. Right, Mr. Merrick?

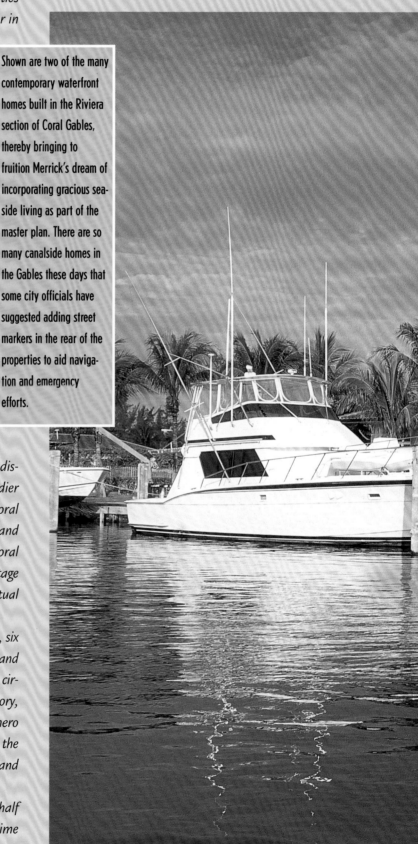

Shown are two of the many contemporary waterfront homes built in the Riviera section of Coral Gables, thereby bringing to fruition Merrick's dream of incorporating gracious seaside living as part of the master plan. There are so many canalside homes in the Gables these days that some city officials have suggested adding street markers in the rear of the properties to aid navigation and emergency efforts.

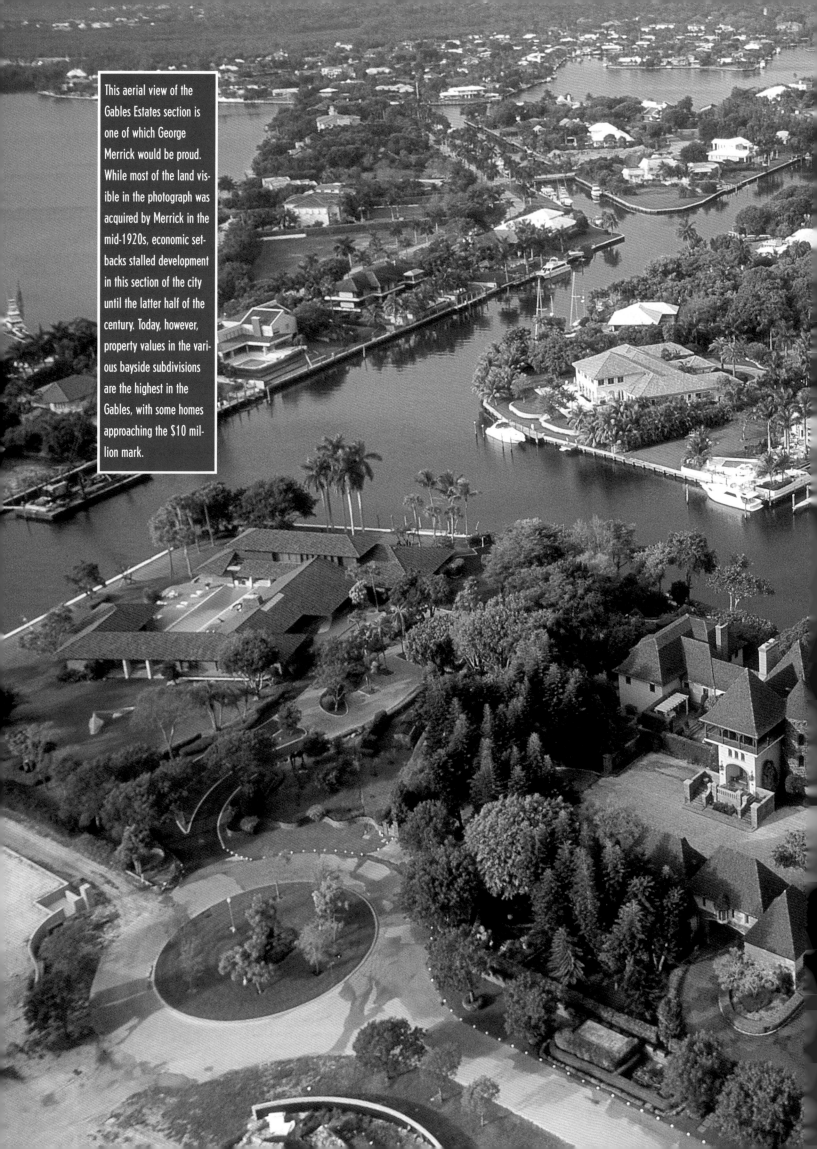

This aerial view of the Gables Estates section is one of which George Merrick would be proud. While most of the land visible in the photograph was acquired by Merrick in the mid-1920s, economic setbacks stalled development in this section of the city until the latter half of the century. Today, however, property values in the various bayside subdivisions are the highest in the Gables, with some homes approaching the $10 million mark.

of building, which can never be secured without restrictions."

Merrick's concerns have persisted with succeeding generations of Coral Gables officials, there is no doubt. The building and zoning regulations are undeniably the most thorough and rigorously enforced in South Florida, perhaps in the country. While such requirements once prompted humorist Dave Barry to note that in Coral Gables, "Most human activity is illegal," Merrick would have calmly replied that his concern was primarily to protect the residents of his community, and that furthermore, he was interested in making a home place for a very broad range of socioeconomic types (in contrast to such upscale developments as Addison Mizner's Palm Beach, for instance, Merrick platted a wide range of residences with building costs

beginning at four thousand dollars and topping out at seventy-five thousand dollars). In a statement that the Three Little Pigs would surely applaud, Merrick insisted, "There is nothing in the Coral Gables restrictions which will prevent the building of a modest home . . . providing it is of stucco."

As has been said, Merrick's vision was a comprehensive and integrated one: he laid out residential sections not only according to design, but to lot size and scope; he designated business and crafts sections; set aside a maintenance and utilities area; distributed hotels and apartments in various parts of the city; assigned areas for country clubs, golf courses, marinas, tennis courts, riding trails, and athletic fields.

In addition to a street system that was intended

Don't Even Think of Speeding Here—Coral Gables' finest assemble for this 1926 photo. BELOW: P. Lehman, director of the Coral Gables Police Department.

—with its impressive entrances, broad vistas, plantings, fountains and plazas—to be aesthetically pleasing, he laid out a system of canals that would provide access to beaches and the sea for inland residents and built a trolley car line that connected his suburb with downtown Miami.

He built a seventy-five-hundred-seat coliseum for public events and booked Will Rogers and his traveling rodeo for its first attraction; he donated land for schools, churches, and civic organizations; he foresaw the value of a university and deeded 160 acres of land along with the necessary

cash to create it; he built Venetian Pool, still one of the largest and most visually striking public pools in existence; and he convinced the Biltmore Corporation to locate its most formidable hotel of the day not far away.

Between 1921, when Merrick began selling lots in his city, and September 1926, when a devastating hurricane ended the initial phase of Coral Gables development, it has been estimated that some $50 million worth of Coral Gables

property had been sold. But it is also said that Merrick had reinvested every dollar he had realized into the constant expansion of his dream.

It all began with the first lot being auctioned by Merrick's Sales Manager Edward E. "Doc" Dammers in November 1921, at an event attended by more than five thousand people. Dammers, who had aided Merrick in the liquidation of his other holdings and whom Edward "Fred" Hartnett, Coral Gables mayor from 1955–1957, called, not unkindly, "a master huckster," enticed lot buyers with free food, transportation, plane rides, build-

ing plans, and other gifts. He and Merrick placed sales offices in New York, Chicago, Atlantic City, Boston, Washington, and other major cities, and purchased a fleet of eighty-six coral pink buses that transported prospects to Coral Gables from Miami and other cities about the state.

Supplementing the efforts of Dammers and a sales corps of some three thousand was a nationwide advertising campaign that swelled to $1 million by 1925, including placements in the *Saturday Evening Post, Forbes, Vogue*, and others. Merrick was the first developer, it is said, to use such popular magazines in this way. There were a host of other promotional endeavors, including the promotional booklets penned by Marjory Stoneman Douglas and Rex Beach, and the hiring of famed attorney and orator William Jennings Bryan, whom Merrick paid one hundred thousand dollars per year—half in property, half in cash—to spread the word.

Bryan delivered speeches at various venues about South Florida including a regular series at the breathtaking Venetian Pool—sometimes from a portable stage, sometimes from a diving platform—and at other special occasions, including an address at the formal opening of the first rapid transit system connecting Coral Gables

LEFT: From the back of a trolley car, William Jennings Bryan welcomes trolly service to Coral Gables on April 30, 1925. ABOVE: Jennings in a rare moment of repose at the Venetian Pool in early 1925. BELOW: Doc Dammers, director of sales for the Coral Gables Corporation, as he looked in the 1920s. Dammers, first mayor of the city, built one of the earliest residences at Coral Way and Columbus Plaza.

with the outside world, in April 1925. Longtime area resident and prominent Miami attorney Alvin Cassell well remembers attending that ribbon-cutting ceremony: "My father took me out to see it all on the trolley line Merrick had built. It seemed a long trip at the time, way out in the boonies as far as we were concerned. Quite a bit had already been built by that time, including the impressive Colonnade there on Coral Way [later Miracle Mile], where Merrick had his offices. But for all that, the notion of a city called Coral Gables seemed very much pie in the sky to most people. This was clear out in the middle of nowhere for those of us from Miami, keep in mind. The most memorable part of that day was listening to William Jennings Bryan. I was only twelve and I don't remember many details of what he said, but I do know that it sounded very important and that it meant a great deal to have him speaking on behalf of Merrick, because one thing remains very clear in my mind: William Jennings Bryan was a very impressive man."

Impressive and highly sought after, Bryan undeniably was. Shortly after that dedication ceremony, Bryan agreed to defend the state of Tennessee in the famous Scopes trial, which established the right to teach the theory of evolution in schools for the first time. While his victory established one of the most significant milestones in legal history, most observers agree that it exacted a heavy toll; Bryan

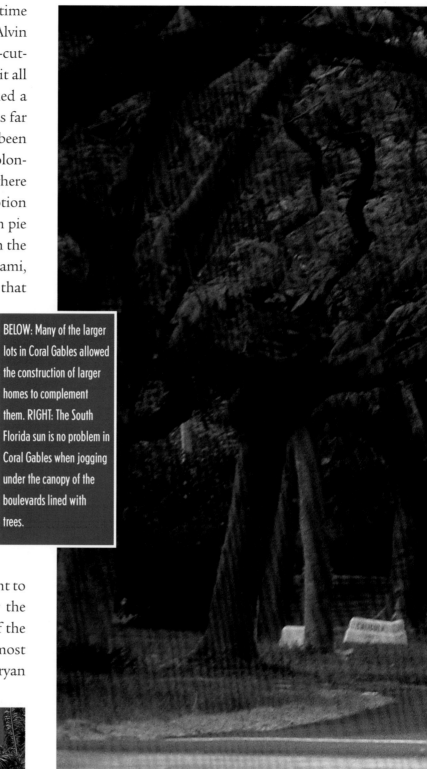

BELOW: Many of the larger lots in Coral Gables allowed the construction of larger homes to complement them. RIGHT: The South Florida sun is no problem in Coral Gables when jogging under the canopy of the boulevards lined with trees.

fell into exhaustion following the trial. Though still in the employ of Merrick, he was never to return to Florida. He died in Tennessee on July 26, 1925.

Meantime, however, Merrick's enterprise continued to flourish. By that time, in addition to the stately Colonnade Building, he had constructed more than one hundred miles of deftly landscaped streets in his new city (one hundred thousand

palms and other plantings had been imported), and two of the eight grand entrances planned by his design team had been completed: the Granada Entrance, on the north, at Granada Boulevard and SW 8th Street (1922), and the Commercial Entrance (1923), on the east, at Alhambra Circle and Douglas Road. Both were designed by his uncle, Denman Fink, who felt that these entrances should function much as the gated portals to the great walled cities of Europe and the Far East. The entrances, he wrote, would serve as a demarcation point where the ordinary world ended, signaling to visitors "that you have come into a place where harmony resides and all discordant elements have been banished."

Marjory Stoneman Douglas added, ". . . to drive about Coral Gables is constantly to be discovering new charms of roadways, new vistas of great

distance, new tunnels of green which open out to light-flooded plazas, new curving perspectives of trees and charming roofs and great lifts of sky." It is also worth noting that Ms. Douglas describes these impressions from the point of view of the motorist, as opposed to the pedestrian. As well-known architectural historian Vincent Scully observes in *Coral Gables: An American Garden City*, Coral Gables was developed as an automotive-oriented suburb, in that its scale required transport of some sort for residents to reach shopping and service districts. If

ABOVE: The first headquarters for the Coral Gables Corporation was located at the southwest corner of Coral Way and Ponce de Leon Boulevard. It is no longer standing. RIGHT: An early view of the Country Club Prado Entrance, the most elaborate and sprawling of the four completed within the city. Designed by Denman Fink and completed in 1927, the entrance includes fountains, a reflecting pool, and a two-hundred-foot-wide, one-and-a-half-mile-long landscaped median extending southward from this point.

that were an inconvenience to residents of the 1920s, however, it may also explain why the beauty of Coral Gables seems so perfectly suited to the automotive age.

It also seems that Merrick was savvy enough to include a bit of everything in his design: while the two earlier-built entrances are modest in comparison to the vast, park-like Country Club Prado (1927), which anchors the northwest corner of the city, and the massive, walled-city effect of the Douglas Entrance (1925–27) in which Supervisory

Architect Phineas Paist had a hand, the Commercial and Granada entrances were (and remain) more approachable in scale, evocative of the humanity and graciousness that Merrick sought for his city.

A city is in fact what Coral Gables had become, receiving its charter from the state of Florida on April 29, 1925. Prior to that time, all governmental affairs had been handled by Merrick's privately held Coral Gables Corporation, of which he was president, and which owned about three-quarters of the land within the city limits.

From an operations standpoint, not a great deal changed immediately. Merrick named Sales Manager Dammers as the first mayor of the city, and appointed other corporation officials to various city posts, including himself and F. Wingfield Webster, corporation executive committee chair, as city commissioners.

Fred Hartnett, who later served as a mayor of Coral Gables, described early city commission meetings this way: "Merrick and his associates would come into the commission chambers, sit down on one side of the table and make their proposals. Then they'd all stand up, go around to the other side of the table and take their seats as city officials, so they could vote upon what had just been set before them."

Such a cozy process would never fly today, of course, but it seems that the goals of Merrick, at least, were primarily those of expediency. "My uncle had impressive offices and he always rode about in a big Lincoln," recalls Donald Kuhn. "And he was very generous, always with a pocketful of dimes to hand out to us kids. The whole family looked to him for support, jobwise, or one way or another." But while he lived comfortably, by all accounts Merrick plowed everything that came his way back into the service of his development.

Even some of the most pragmatic decisions of his team paid great benefits to the community at large. Fred Hartnett liked to tell the story of Dammers sitting at a table in the Coral Gables Country Club with several of his associates at the end of a particularly frenetic sales day, listening as one salesman complained about the difficulty he'd

Venetian Casino

CORAL GABLES

THE VENETIAN pool of Coral Gables not only focvses, with its broad green lagoons, its shady porticos and vine covered loggias, its great Spanish towers, its tea rooms and dance floor and dressing rooms, the leisvred life of a whole region, bvt it provides all America with a vniqve new architectvral development which will certainly set a new example for fvtvre bvilders. ~ ~ ~ ~ ~ ~ ~ ~ ~

had in convincing a prospect to buy a lot that bordered on a quarry, where a good deal of oolite had been excavated for many of the early homes built in Coral Gables.

"It's an eyesore," the salesman complained. "We'll never sell the lots around there."

Dammers nodded thoughtfully, but he wasn't necessarily agreeing with the man. According to Hartnett, it wasn't long before Dammers had come up with the solution. The next day, Denman Fink and Phineas Paist were hard at work, transforming his proposal into reality. What their efforts produced we call today the Venetian Pool, a sixty-thousand-square-foot, eight-hundred-thousand-gallon swimming pool (a typical backyard pool might contain fifteen thousand gallons), the only structure of its type to be listed in the National Register of Historic Places.

To refer to the Venetian as a "swimming pool" somehow does not do it justice, for Denman Fink and Phineas Paist conspired to transform that

An assembled throng listens to the Jan Garber Orchestra at Venetian Pool, shortly after its opening in 1924. The pool was often pressed into service as an entertainment arena.

An assembled throng listens to the Jan Garber Orchestra at Venetian Pool, shortly after its opening in 1924. The pool was often pressed into service as an entertainment arena.

Today, the Venetian Pool is the only public swimming pool in the country listed in the National Register of Historic Places. With its meandering shoreline, caves, waterfalls, island, bridge, and beach, it is a never-ending source of delight for adults and children alike.

RIGHT: "Venetian" bathing beauties, c. 1925. FAR RIGHT: The Venetian Pool is open virtually year round, attracting over 200,000 visitors a year. The tower in the background now houses the pool's offices, but was formerly used as an observation post.

abandoned rock pit into a mind-boggling vision of Venice dropped down in the South Florida tropics. The pool itself is a vast, irregularly shaped lagoon, containing waterfalls, coral rock diving platforms, a palm-studded island, caves and grottoes, all encompassed by lush tropical plantings and a sandy beach. The surrounding buildings, which house locker rooms and other service facilities, are done in typical Mediterranean Revival fancy, with soaring observation towers capped by the familiar barrel-tiled roofs framing a spacious loggia, which in turn shelters a children's wading pool. The structures feature painted murals, carved balustrades, ornamental ironwork and lighting fixtures, along with Venetian-inspired bridges and accompanying piers. The open-air courtyard contains touches typical of Fink, especially his ability to create the illusion of antiquity in Gables styling: fountains, intricately scrolled tile work, plaster walls aged overnight by application of oxides (and in some cases, animal compost, to encourage the growth of moss and mildew), layered applications of washes to simulate fading, even the deliberate misapplication of plaster to simulate the crumbling of the ages and the resultant exposure of the underlying brick.

Though the finer points of Fink's handiwork might escape them, there is no doubt that were a committee of children invited to describe the swimming pool of their dreams, the Venetian Pool would be it. The place enhanced property values for Merrick, it is true, but far more important, has entranced generations of South Florida families ever since it was completed in December 1924. It remains tops on the list when residents are directing visitors toward the sights one must see.

The Venetian Pool did serve its makers well, of course. An eyesore had been transformed into an asset in more ways than one. Prospects rode those coral pink buses directly to the Venetian Pool, where their first impressions of this new city

116

would be formed, by the splendorous fever dream before them, but also by the hypnotic opening address on Florida boom times and progress delivered there by William Jennings Bryan, the Silver-Tongued Orator himself. From that dizzying experience it would be back onto the bus to view what prime properties might still be available for the quick thinking and quick-to-act. After, it would be on to the elegantly appointed Coral Gables Country Club for lunch and the chance to digest prospects that had been laid out like markings on a treasure map. For those who needed more time and more urging—or perhaps as a reward for the happy buyer—there might be another trip back to the Venetian Pool that same evening to view an aquatics exhibition by Esther Williams or Johnny Weissmuller.

Sometimes, those returning for an evening visit would find that the entire pool had been drained and transformed into an amphitheater for a more

however, and in 1987, the city undertook a $2 million renovation that converted the pool to filtered operation and restored many of the ravages of time. The result is what historian Vincent Scully has called "without question the most delightful public swimming pool ever built anywhere."

The fact that for many years the Venetian Pool served as the site of swimming competitions for the local high schools and the University of Miami is a reminder that a number of George Merrick's endeavors could hardly be construed as profit-making in nature. As early as 1915, there had been discussion among South Florida community leaders concerning the need for a "Pan-American University," which any forward-looking community would need as a foundation for its future. But Merrick was the first to do something about it.

From the beginning, Merrick had included a university in the plans for his city, and early in 1925, he announced a slate of regents that included William Jennings Bryan. At that time he also pledged $5 million to make the University of Miami a reality, one destined in Merrick's words, "to become the cultural center of the entire South." Merrick had considered several sites for the campus, including the land where the Biltmore Hotel now sits, and

ambitious address by Bryan, or an orchestra concert by Jan Garber, Paul Whiteman or other notables of the day. While such an undertaking might seem the height of excess to the modern observer, the fact is that the Venetian was operated until 1986 as a filterless, "drain and fill" pool, with every one of those eight hundred thousand gallons drained nightly and replaced with unchlorinated water from underground artesian wells. Environmental and health concerns eventually prevailed,

another near the intersection of Red Road and Coral Way. But in the end he settled on the present site, adjacent to what is now U.S. 1, in large part due to the presence of a lake thereon that the newly appointed Board of Regents felt would "act very beautifully as a reflecting pool for the Court of Honor of our main building as contemplated by our architect."

The latter was a reference to plans already conceived by Denman Fink, Phineas Paist, and Paul

Chalfin for the main administration building. Their design also made provision for buildings for liberal arts, engineering, law, medicine, music, art, and others, and included an imposing president's home, all of it done in the characteristic Mediterranean Revival style. There was to be a gymnasium, a chapel, a library, an athletic field, swimming pools, and—modern-day Hurricanes fans, take note—a stadium.

The cornerstone for the administration building

M-28—Merrick Building
University of Miami, Fla.

The Merrick Building is shown here under construction on the new campus of the University of Miami in 1926. A hurricane and subsequent economic woes would delay completion of the structure, originally designed in the characteristic Palace of the Doges style, for more than twenty years. ABOVE LEFT: The postcard shows what planners had in mind for the University of Miami while the other postcard (above) shows what actually was built some years later.

MIAMI UNIVERSITY
CORAL GABLES, FLA.
CORAL GABLES CONSTRUCTION
& SUPPLY CO., BUILDERS
PHINEAS E. PAIST, ARCHITECT
DENMAN FINK, ASSOCIATE
NO.   DATE 6-7-26

RIGHT: William J. Bryan extols the virtues of Coral Gables life during ground-breaking ceremonies for the Biltmore Hotel in 1925. BELOW: Shown here is the cover sheet for the unofficial city song, "When the Moon Shines in Coral Gables," much performed during the glory days of the city's development. It was played more than once on the night of the Biltmore Hotel's gala opening, when three orchestras performed simultaneously for over two thousand guests, including three hundred dignitaries from New York City, who arrived by special train: "The Miami-Biltmore Express." The city's official song is now "Coral Gables, City Beautiful," penned by Vera Gallogly Harcourt, and adopted by the Coral Gables commission in 1983.

was set in February 1926, and at that ceremony—where the building was dedicated to Merrick's father, Solomon—George Merrick revealed something of his deeper feelings: "I am tremendously proud to have a hand in this great thing, and I pledge now and through the years the best that is in me to its upbuilding. Proud as I am of what has been accomplished for Miami in Coral Gables, I am prouder of this University beginning than of everything else put together."

The year 1926 was to serve as the best of times and later as the worst of times for Merrick. Not only had he begun construction on his cherished University, he also witnessed the manifestation of his most ambitious commercial undertaking, the opening of the Miami-Biltmore Hotel. That Merrick was able to convince the most prestigious firm of the day to locate the costliest hotel it had ever built on an inland site in South Florida was all by itself a tribute to the power of his vision.

From the earliest days of his project, Merrick had considered a sizable resort hotel a necessary aspect of his plans. As one reporter for the *Miami News* put it, "Mr. Merrick saw the need of a great hotel in Coral Gables, a hotel which would not only serve as a complete hostelry to the crowds which were thronging to Coral Gables, but would also serve as a center of sports and fashion . . . ."

Merrick had also become enthralled with the Giralda Tower during a visit to the Cathedral of Seville, and had in fact dispatched his own architect to Spain to study the original, so that it could be incorporated into the design for his dream hotel.

Then, in 1924, Merrick met with John McEntee Bowman and soon convinced him of the glory (and the profit, one presumes) to be gained in Coral Gables. In late November, the *Miami Herald* carried the story: Bowman-Biltmore Hotels would spend $10 million to build a hotel and resort complex, including three golf courses, polo fields, a tennis court, and a swimming pool without parallel.

Bowman insisted upon his own team of architects, Leonard Schultze and S. Fullerton Weaver, who were well versed in the opulent style of the day. Schultze had designed the Gothic-encrusted Grand Central Station, and he and Weaver had collaborated on a number of Renaissance-inspired structures, including the Los Angeles and Atlanta Biltmore Hotels. Merrick, who had kept Martin L. Hampton in Spain for more than three months trying to come up with a design that would be workable for something in the neighborhood of $1.25 million, did not hesitate. In Bowman, he had found a

Alex Smith, the first pro of the Miami-Biltmore Country Club, lines up a putt as work continues on the Schultze-Weaver clubhouse behind him. Prospective members were asked to pony up $1,500 in initiation fees and $300 in annual dues.

123

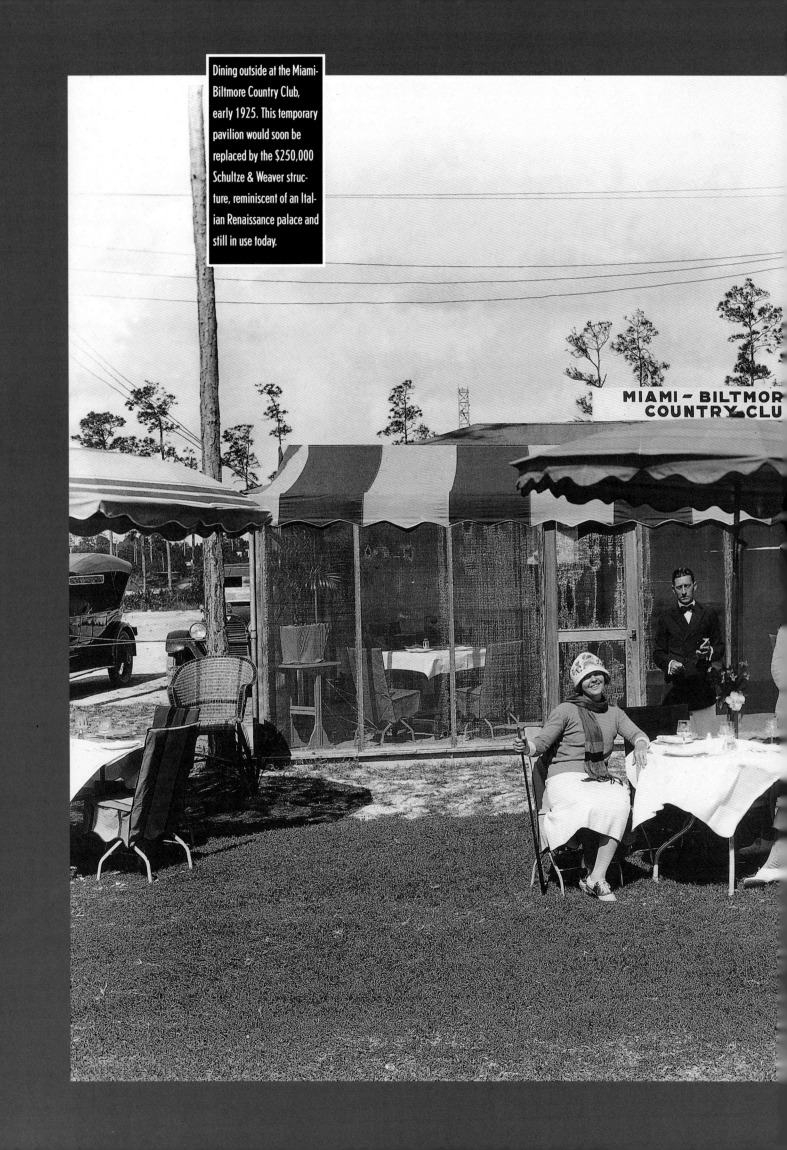

Dining outside at the Miami-Biltmore Country Club, early 1925. This temporary pavilion would soon be replaced by the $250,000 Schultze & Weaver structure, reminiscent of an Italian Renaissance palace and still in use today.

MIAMI – BILTMOR
COUNTRY CLU

nected to the Coral Gables Waterway and then to Biscayne Bay itself, Merrick set about the construction of a beachside recreation area that he called Tahiti Beach. He trucked in vast quantities of sand, erected a band shell and dancing pavilion, and placed about the shores an elaborate series of thatched huts meant to conjure up visions of a South Seas paradise. It was a pleasure dome where, a publicity flier promised, "discriminating people will find their own kind."

Meantime, a few miles upstream, more than one

man who would spend $10 million of his own money, price no object, and provide Coral Gables with a replica of the Tower of Sevilla itself, 315 feet in height.

Martin L. Hampton, as we say, became history. Merrick was to explain something of his thinking later, in this story from the *Miami Daily News and Metropolis* describing the hotel's opening: "Putting it in practical Miami language, I believe, consciously or unconsciously, almost every man will dig up more dollars for or work harder to retain, the piece of ground that has in its neighborhood the inspiration of such beauty as great towers like the Cox tower [of the *Miami News* Building] or this Biltmore tower can yield."

The hotel and its tower were only part of Merrick's ever-evolving plan. He had also come to realize the tremendous drawing power of ocean access and waterfront building sites for his clientele, and in 1925 had added the six-thousand-acre Riviera district to his holdings, bringing the total under development to some ten thousand acres, and at last linking his landlocked city to the sea. While it was his intention to one day build a one-thousand-room hotel and European-styled casino complex on his newly purchased bayfront property (he had already begun talks with Bowman on that score), Merrick had come up with an interim plan, yet one more flamboyant stroke upon an already jaw-dropping canvas.

Figuring that he was about to have a hotel up and running on the banks of a canal that con-

ABOVE: The grand lobby of the Miami-Biltmore Hotel in 1926. RIGHT: Among the celebrities at the opening of the Biltmore Hotel were Gene Tunney (second from left) and golf champion Bobby Jones (second from right). On Jones's right is Charles Flynn, the first manager of the hotel.

thousand workers were hard at work on the Biltmore and its associated amenities, transforming an area where Merrick pointed out, "eight years ago I was growing tomatoes." The Country Club building, done in the style of an Italian Renaissance palace, was completed by April 1925, along with two eighteen-hole golf courses designed by Donald Ross, stables, and riding paths. Grey foxes—the descendants of which still roam the area, feeding on the offerings of area residents, and the occasional house cat—were imported for the hunt.

Ground was broken on the hotel itself in March, and work continued at a frenetic pace throughout the year, culminating in a formal opening in January 1926, an event the likes of which South Florida had never before experienced. The physical immensity and grandeur of the building was enough in itself to capture the imagination of the public: 350 rooms altogether, with a fifteen-story tower rising from a ten-story center block, and two massive seven-story wings jutting from that centerpiece, lavishly embellished with traditional Mediterreanean

Taken February 27, 1925, at the Miami-Biltmore Hotel, this was just one of the many group photos that visitors posed for. The hotel employed numerous measures to attract guests, and they all came away singing the Biltmore's praises.

furnishings, rugs, and drapes alone worth $1 million.

Two deluxe trains jammed with more than one thousand celebrities, media representatives, and others in the thrall of Merrick's vision rushed down from New York City to Miami in less than thirty-six hours, a new speed record for the time. The guest list was a wild amalgam of socialite and celebrity, including Eddie Rickenbacker, Cornelius Vanderbilt Jr., Gene Sarazen, Bobby Jones, Bernard Baruch, Gene Tunney, Adolph Zukor, Tex

Ricard, and many more. There were five thousand requests to attend the opening dinner dance, which had a capacity of fifteen-hundred. Three bands were pressed into service to cope with the crowds that night, and the next day twenty-five thousand people arrived for tours and perhaps a glimpse of the New York models, sporting the latest in gowns, furs, and jewelry.

If the Venetian Pool was huge, the Biltmore's pool—with Director of Aquatic Instruction, Johnny Weissmuller—had gone one better: built to hold

1,250,000 gallons of water and encompassing twenty thousand square feet in all, it was the nation's largest. Those who insisted upon frolicking in salt water could stroll across a fairway's breadth to a canal landing where they might board one of twenty-five gondolas imported from Venice, along with their gondoliers, who would transport them down the Coral Gables Waterway where all the pleasures of Tahiti Beach awaited.

The Biltmore was, and remains, the grandest physical monument to Merrick's earthly aspirations. The tower, visible from as far away as downtown Miami, and serving as a point of reference for mariners on Biscayne Bay, commands its domain like an enormous exclamation point. Residents orient themselves by it, and golfers, real and imagined, have long found themselves inspired by its accomplishment. The exquisite scene was recalled in the novel, *Deal on Ice*, in which this author described a golfer as he teed up at the Biltmore: "Its lights were fairly glowing now, twilight fully fallen, and it looked like nothing you'd ever see in Nebraska. He was glad their work had brought them out this way. Coconut Grove had its pleasures, but this was something else."

At the time of the Biltmore's completion, no aspect of Merrick's dream seemed impossible, no prospect

beyond reach. The spirits of the country soared, fueled by fumes from the Jazz Age and juiced by the happy tale from Wall Street's ticker. Paradisaical Florida —particularly South Florida and Coral Gables—seemed the perfect place to stash those profits, or speculate for more, or, at the very least, enjoy the fruits of all those gains. "My candle burns at both ends;/ It will not last the night," went a popular poem of the day, penned by Edna St. Vincent Millay. "But ah, my foes, and oh, my friends—/ it gives a lovely light!"

There were signs of trouble on the horizon, of course: certain sober-sided banking interests in the Midwest were concerned with rampant land speculation in untried Florida developments. They had even gone so far as to take out advertisements in northern newspapers warning of the dangers posed by those who operated like the "binder boys," infamous agents who bound land contracts for 10 percent down, then sold and resold the same contracts many times over, often in the course of a single day. This inflating land prices far beyond anything consistent with their value. Such

Huntsmen and well-wishers gather on the patio of the Miami-Biltmore Country Club in 1932, just prior to the chase.

publications as the *New York Times* had picked up on the story and conducted their own investigations warning investors of the potential dangers.

But Merrick had reason to believe that these were only the squawks to be expected from the Chicken Little crowd: those who lacked the vision or the courage to invest in the future.

After all, it was at about the same time that banker and former Ohio Governor Myers Y. Cooper approached him with a proposal to develop the series of villages in Coral Gables. Merrick would agree to adopt a secondary position on his ownership in the building sites, and the American Building Corporation would use the resulting equity to finance their ambitious project—the $75 million undertaking that would become the fourteen planned villages of Coral Gables.

In covering the Biltmore's opening in 1926, the *New York Times* reported to the nation that in five short years Coral Gables had been transformed from nothingness into a thriving city of sixteen square miles with a population of more than seventy-five hundred. Nearly twenty-eight hundred homes and apartments, housing some twenty-one hundred families, had risen from the pine barrens and guava groves. There were half a dozen hotels in addition to the Biltmore, a burgeoning business section with banks and a post office, churches, Woman's and Gardening Clubs, two Country Clubs, three golf courses, two grammar schools, a military academy, a Catholic seminary, a boarding school for girls, the University High School, and the University of Miami under way. The seventy-five-hundred-seat Coliseum had been completed, as had the Venetian Pool, with the magnificent De Soto fountain, the rival of many a European counterpart, just steps away. Merrick enjoyed the backing of one of the most esteemed corporate interests in the United States and was engaged in a mammoth undertaking with a consortium of Midwestern bankers. What could go wrong?

The answer, of course: Everything.

PART THREE

Busted...and Reborn

NE OF THE BRIEFER, more prophetic poems in George Merrick's 1920 collection goes this way:

> *Gray-purple dust behind the wrath-swept hill:—*
> *An out-lined broken oak; black, lone, once tall.*
> *Drear tragic figure, —bowed by awful will-*
> *Transfixed against the fading, fateful pall.*

"After the Hurricane" it is entitled, and while it was written and published well before the first spadeful of earth was ever turned in Coral Gables, the poem stands as eerie presentiment of what would befall Merrick and his dream.

In many ways, things in 1926 could not have seemed better. Sales figures, both commercial and residential, had never been higher. Assessed property values neared the $100 million mark, and Merrick claimed that more than $150 million had been spent in development altogether. There were over 100 miles of paved streets and another 125 of sidewalks criss-crossing the 16 square miles of its territory. A trolley line now linked the area with downtown Miami, making travel from the distant suburb a much more practical matter.

LEFT: The Coral Gables skyline has changed dramatically over the years, but the vast majority of the city has retained its original Mediterranean flavor.
BELOW: Golf in Coral Gables has been one of the main drawing cards for the city since the 1920s.

Coral Gables Congregational Church, 3010 De Soto Boulevard, near the Biltmore Hotel, was the first church built in the city, completed in 1925 on land donated by George Merrick in memory of his father Solomon, a Congregational minister. Still a popular house of worship, the church also serves as a community center in other respects as well, often hosting concerts and appearances by visiting dignitaries and authors, including Nadine Gordimer, Isabella Rosselini, and many others.

countered by enumerating many of the accomplishments of the Gables in a lengthy *New York Times* interview earlier that year, capping his argument with typical bravado: "The lure of the tropics is a great and definite thing alone to build upon. The Miami area comprises absolutely the only American tropics, and in that great fact, Miami owns and will forever hold a priceless American monopoly . . . ."

Ironically enough, it was one of the very aspects

The lavish opening of the Biltmore had brought unprecedented national attention to the development. Coral Gables had become an incorporated city, with its own mayor and city commission, and some $8 million in bond offerings had been floated to finance various city improvements. Tallman Hospital had opened, as had a pair of banks. For recreation, the two country clubs provided for ample golf, and there were also riding paths, and an exotic public beach. Eight religious congregations had been organized, and the elegant Congregational Church, fronting the Biltmore Hotel, had been open for more than a year.

In addition to a military academy, St. Joseph's Academy for Girls, and a number of private elementary schools, Coral Gables Elementary School had opened, as had Ponce de Leon High School, the latter already enrolling 10 percent of the total high school population in Dade County. Construction had begun upon the crowning jewel of the community, the University of Miami. In many respects, Merrick's dream had become a reality; furthermore, it had become so within the span of just five years.

Still, there were signs of trouble on the horizon. Rampant land speculation in Florida and the practices of unscrupulous developers and sales agents had fueled the suspicions of more conservative banking groups in the Midwest and Northeast. These bankers had been lobbying for the passage of "blue-sky" laws restricting investments and had placed full-page newspaper advertisements warning of the dangers in ill-advised Florida land speculation. Merrick

ABOVE: St. Joseph's Academy, pictured here under construction in the heyday of the 1920s, later became St. Theresa School, a coeducational, K-8 institution still operating at 2701 Indian Mound Trail, near the Church of the Little Flower. RIGHT: "Indeed, there is much to enrich the dignity of home life and community spirit everywhere in Coral Gables"— George Merrick, 1926. Young worshippers at Coral Gables Congregational Church prepare for a special Christmas pageant.

of tropical living that was to prove Merrick's undoing. While ever ready to point out the advantages of his site—"comparatively high elevation, healthful and comfortable living all the year round, unsurpassed drinking water and fertile soil"—and quick to extol the virtues of the local climate "of summer the whole year through," Merrick, who went so far as to proclaim the "lack of humidity" in the City Beautiful, had overlooked a far more cataclysmic scourge that nearly all residents of the Caribbean Rim must periodically endure.

Hurricane, the lash is termed, and on September 18, 1926, it was to fall upon the residents of Coral Gables and South Florida with terrible and unexpected fury. While the weather bureau had predicted the approach of the storm as early as September 16 and local newspapers had carried warnings on the following day, local residents were resolutely unalarmed. A hundred-mile-an-

The Church of the Little Flower is located at 1265 Anastasia Avenue. It was designed by G. M. Barry and F. O. Kay and completed in 1951, to replace the original church sanctuary that was built in 1927 by one of the eight major congregations organized during the earliest days of the city.

hour storm had delivered a glancing blow to Miami in July of that year and damage had been slight. As a consequence, news of this second storm's approach provoked little more than shrugs.

Shortly after midnight on September 18th, however, the winds began to blow in earnest. They were soon to become a gale that would carry on through the night with a freight-train roar that blew out doors and windows (including nearly every pane in the Biltmore's grand tower) and made the earlier July storm seem a harmless breeze in comparison. When the hurricane finally began to abate, many residents stumbled out (or stared up through splintered roofs) into the early light, stunned by the massive devastation wrought by the direct strike of a major storm.

And yet, things were about to get worse. As they gaped at the wreckage about them, some noticed that the sky was darkening ominously and that the winds were picking up again, this time from the opposite direction. The calm that residents had wandered out into was only the eye of the great storm passing over. In the words of one resident, as quoted by Kathryne Ashley, "We barely had time to reach the house when such a fury struck as I can not tell about or words describe."

The winds had reached 128 miles per hour by the time the last gauge blew away, and were estimated to have reached 140 miles per hour at their peak, marking a catastrophic Category IV storm by today's standards. Bayside structures not already devastated by the first assault were submerged, flattened and washed away like tinder by the tidal surge brought ashore by the shifted winds. "Miami is Wiped Out," read the headlines of several newspapers across the nation. Some 114 people had died in the storm's onslaught, and the property damage was incalculable. Every downtown building in Miami suffered major damage. Miami Beach was literally washed away.

Coral Gables, as a result of Merrick's strict building standards and its relatively protected setting, fared somewhat better. Windows and roofs were lost, the awnings were ripped away, and the fabled trees and shrubs had been blown to kingdom come. But most structures remained intact.

The Man Behind the Myth

George E. Merrick was, by all accounts, a rare blend of the practical and the visionary: a businessman with the soul of a poet, a land developer who was also an environmentalist. Had there been more like him in the early days of Florida's growth, were there more of his like today, who knows how many delightful suburbs would stand in the place of undifferentiated sprawl.

Asked to characterize the "real" man behind the legendary accomplishments, nephew Donald Kuhn pauses, then provides a few tidbits:

"He was smart, of course. His sister Helen called him 'Old Hundred' because that's the score he always got on his school work. And he was clearly destined to make something of himself: his sister Ethel called him 'The Great I-Am.' But he wasn't really conceited, and he was always good to his family. He did have a temper, though. All the Merricks had short fuses, in fact. After my stepfather died, Uncle George stepped in to help. He footed the bill to send me and my two brothers to a boarding school run by the Seventh Day Adventists up in Maitland [near Orlando]. I was just fourteen and got to missing my mother pretty bad. So I sneaked away from school one morning and hitchhiked all the way down to Miami. It took most of the day. When I finally did get home, I found out my mother had moved and nobody knew where. I didn't have any choice but to go to my Uncle George's house. He was living out on Flagler Street by then.

"So I knocked on the door and Uncle George answered. He took one look at me and asked, 'Does the school know you're here?'"

Kuhn smiles at this point. "I got all the way to 'No, but . . .' when the screen door flew open and there he came after me, steam pouring out his ears. I took off down Flagler Street with Uncle George hot on my tail, ready to tan me. He'd gotten kind of portly by then, though, and I was pretty fast. He never

did catch me, and I sure didn't go back. I slept the night huddled on a bench in the Douglas Arch and hitchhiked back to school the next day. He'd already called and told them to be on the lookout for me. No more fooling around for me. After that, I stayed put."

Tallman Hospital had survived; its thirty-bed capacity swelled to 150 in the aftermath. The Coral Gables Golf and Country Club, buffered by the neighboring Biltmore Tower, had also held up well enough to become an emergency soup kitchen, providing some two thousand meals a day for needy residents.

Perhaps the most devastating physical blow was dealt to the site of the fledgling University of Miami. Construction on the main building, which had reached a particularly vulnerable stage, was re-duced to a shambles.

Nonetheless, residents were resilient, with headlines such as those in the *Miami News* typical: "Optimism, born of the will to do, reigns." Miami Mayor Ed Romfh promulgated the slo-gan "Miami by the Sea is Ready" for the upcoming tourist season. The Univer-sity of Miami took over the Anastasia Hotel (which had never opened) and the San Sebastian Hotel (intended to be used to house employees of the Coral Gables Corpora-tion) and managed to open for classes on October 18.

TOP: Biscayne Bay at sunset. RIGHT: The rich colors of Coral Gables architecture always make a grand state-ment.

Merrick was as optimistic as ever, arguing that the hurricane had dealt the city only a temporary setback. He pushed on with a number of projects into 1927, including the completion of the massive Douglas Entrance and the picturesque Coral Gables City Hall, which began construction in November 1927 and was opened in February 1928 (the original city hall building still stands at 303 Alhambra Circle, and is used as the Coral Gables post of the American Legion). Merrick also donated club room space in the new Douglas Entrance for a public library, adding furniture and tapestries he had imported from Spain, and saw to it that the city commission appropriated one thousand dollars for books.

But so far as business was concerned, Merrick was fighting a tide almost as formidable as that tossed up by the hurricane of 1926. While a few projects devastated by the storm were completed, more had their developers simply walk away. An increasing number of purchasers began to default on their land payments. Lenders, especially those already made leery by the bad press that had pre-ceded the storm, pulled in lines of credit. Miami historian Arva Moore Parks reported that by 1928, "For the first time in the city's short history, more people were leaving than arriving."

Still, given Merrick's indefatigable nature and the innate appeal of Coral Gables itself, the cycles of public confidence might have been outlasted. But then came another unfor-seen catastrophe: the stock market crash of 1929. The Coral Gables Corporation, already reeling, was forced into bankruptcy. Merrick, who had lost favor with a number of associates and was forced from his city commissioner's seat, liquidated per-sonal assets to pay his debts and com-mitments. His days as a major developer and political player in Coral Gables had come to an end—as had the fairy-tale era for the city itself.

Of course, the saga does not end at this juncture. By 1929, Coral Gables had lived a scant four years as a city, and only eight years as a concept in its founder's eye.

Merrick had much left to do. Not long after his ouster from the day-to-day affairs of his beloved city, he was hard at work on another project, the development of a fishing resort on Matecumbe Key, which he called Carribee Colony. Merrick, who had lost his home in the Gables, took up resi-dence on Flagler Street and opened a realty office near the Colonnade Building in Coral Gables. He

spent a fair amount of time in the Keys but, according to his nephew Donald Kuhn, was not about to move far from his Gables roots.

Yet another hurricane, the fabled storm of 1935—which killed hundreds of World War I veterans laboring on the overseas highway as it blew through the Florida Keys—was to wipe out Carribee Colony. Merrick, who had been the mainstay of his family, whether by providing his siblings with jobs or financial assistance, took the setback in stride. According to Kuhn, Merrick was only sorry that his ability to help his family had been so severely curtailed.

"I never heard him complain," Kuhn says. "And I truly don't think he was ever depressed by his reversals. He had his critics, but essentially he ignored them. Mostly, he was proud of what he had accomplished, and I think most of us would understand why."

Merrick became a member of the Dade County Zoning Commission in 1935 and served as the chairman of that body until 1939. He was appointed postmaster of the city of Miami in 1940 by Sen. Claude Pepper, a position he held until his death in 1942. "He might have died broke, but he wasn't broken," Kuhn says. "I don't think he particularly liked being postmaster—it didn't suit his outgoing nature. He was a big handsome man, with big hands and a great booming voice. He was convinced he could rebuild right to the end."

As for Merrick's faith in Coral Gables, Kuhn says that it never flagged. Right on through the 1930s, Kuhn recalls, Merrick would pick up his mother to go for an ice cream, then ride about the

town, to look at whatever might be being built. "He lived and breathed Coral Gables," Kuhn says. "And he had a great sense of humor. He liked to say that 'one day, there'll be a million people living down here.' And I'd say, 'What'll they eat, Uncle George?' And he'd laugh and say, 'Each other.'"

In those grim 1930s when the country was locked in the Great Depression, it would have

taken great faith indeed to foresee 1,000,000 residents in the Miami and Coral Gables area. While the population of Miami hovered at about 100,000 in 1930, the 10,000 residents of Coral Gables had dwindled by nearly half, to 5,697. Nearly 3,000 homes had been built in the first ten years of Gables history; only three were built in 1932. These were the days of lonely bike rides described by Tom Thorpe, down unpaved streets,

past unfinished home sites and vacant lots.

But as attorney Alvin Cassell recalls, things didn't seem so bad in South Florida, comparatively speaking. "You have to remember," he says, "our depression began in 1926. We'd had plenty of time to get used to it. We were learning to get along by the time the rest of the country was just feeling the worst of it."

Nearby Miami kept itself alive as a tourist

ABOVE: Golf has always been a popular draw at the Biltmore, as evidenced by this 1932 photograph of club champions. RIGHT: The interior of the two-floor Everglades Suite at the Biltmore Hotel, named for the murals of scenes from the Everglades that grace its walls. It is also sometimes referred to as the Al Capone Suite, for a former guest who reputedly lived there in another era. More recent guests have included movie stars and U.S. presidents.

destination by maintaining an easygoing attitude toward booze and gambling. At the height of Prohibition, the city had earned a reputation as the rum-running capital of the nation, due in part to its proximity to Bimini, its ragged, difficult-to-patrol coastline and also to the disregard of local authorities for an unpopular federal policy. Even Coral Gables figured in this drama, with Merrick's touted "forty miles of waterfront" and network of canals providing convenient points of entry for the souped-up, Cigarette-prototype speedboats of the smugglers.

Speakeasies were found everywhere in the metro area, and freestanding gambling casinos such as the Royal Palm and the Colonial Inn dotted the coastline from Government Cut in downtown Miami all the way north to 163rd Street, where Russell Graveley's China Doll enticed out-of-town visitors to try their hands at everything from slots to roulette to baccarat. "You'd have never known he was a gambler to look at him," Alvin Cassell says of Graveley, whom he describes as a suave, impeccably dressed but sedate man. "I went into his place once and saw all these men in tuxedos and women in gowns playing the tables. We went into

ABOVE: Bathing Beauties at the Biltmore, c. 1938. Despite the economic problems afflicting Coral Gables as a whole, the Biltmore continued to flourish as a tourist destination well into the 1930s, and its huge swimming pool was often used as a site for various pageants. RIGHT: Pardon Me Boys: Wounded G.I.s find fancy digs in which to recuperate when the Biltmore Hotel is commandeered as a hospital by the U.S. War Department during World War II.

Russell's office and I remarked that business seemed to be doing all right, for the depression. Russell smiled and leaned forward. 'I'll tell you something, Alvin,' he said. 'Every one of those people is a shill.'"

Cassell adds that Graveley, as did most casino operators, made it a policy to exclude locals from participating in the gaming. It was a practice that, along with substantial payoffs to local authorities, was to account for the strong support of gambling activities by the local populace, who believed that South Florida needed the attraction of the casinos to survive.

Local legislators championed bills legalizing betting on jai alai, and horse and dog racing, measures that still stand. For a brief time in 1934, even slot machines were legalized.

Even the Biltmore traded on Miami's wide-open image to keep its doors open long after most Coral Gables hostelries had fallen on hard times. The hotel, which served as a shelter for some twenty-two hundred homeless people in the aftermath of the 1926 hurricane, underwent renovation soon after the storm, and, with its splendid furnishings, its vast pool and tennis courts, bridle paths, and thirty-six holes of golf, continued to operate and to attract a celebrity-studded clientele.

These were the years that Al Capone had taken up residence in Miami; from 1928 until 1932, when he was convicted of income tax fraud and sent to prison, he maintained a mansion on Palm Island and was a frequent guest at the Biltmore, often hosting legendary parties on the lavishly appointed thirteenth-floor rooms still referred at times as the "Capone Suite." In this rarefied setting, liquor flowed freely there for the guests of the legendary mobster, and casino-styled gambling flourished, high above the reach of any sober-sided authority.

Though the Biltmore was forced into receivership at the time of the collapse of the Coral Gables Corporation in April 1929, its operation had been uninterrupted: the property was transferred to bondholders for a few months, until John Bowman, the president of Bowman-Biltmore, was able to put together an ownership group including former New York Governor Al Smith. Bowman's group purchased the hotel, originally ballyhooed as a $10 million project, for $2.1 million, and operated it until 1931, when they sold to Henry Doherty, chairman and founder of Cities Service Company.

Doherty had a unique concept for revitalizing the Biltmore. At the same time, he had purchased the Roney Plaza on Miami Beach and the Angler's Club in Key Largo, forming what he called the Florida Year Round Club. He pumped money into the renovation of all the properties, including sixty thousand dollars to upgrade the Biltmore's golf courses and embarked upon a national advertising campaign offering a round of beachfront, fishing, and golfing activities that would entice tourists throughout all seasons. Doherty sponsored the annual ten-thousand-dollar Miami Biltmore Open, then the richest golf tournament on tour, and continued to bring in big-name bands and aquatic performers. Guests in the Doherty Days were as glamorous as ever—the names of Ginger Rogers, Deanna Durbin, Judy Garland, Bing Crosby, Wendell Wilkie, and Rudy Vallee dotted the register.

Such maneuvering kept the Biltmore alive through the 1930s, but Doherty died in 1939, and in late 1942, the U.S. War Department commandeered the facility (as it did nearly all Miami area hotels at the time) to use as a dormitory for army training recruits and shortly thereafter as a hospital.

The once-grand flagship of the Biltmore chain was gutted, its chandeliers replaced by institutional lighting, its ceiling murals covered with acoustical tile, its grand ballrooms and public areas chopped into wallboard cubicles. Its French doors were replaced by fireproof steel barriers replete with breaker bars. The pool was drained, the grand restaurants with Tiffany place settings had been converted to cafeteria operations, and the country club was shuttered.

Big names still checked into its rooms. Dwight D. Eisenhower was a patient. Famous name entertainers, including Bob Hope, Al Jolson, Danny Kaye, Sophie Tucker, and Jane Russell, still dropped by, though this time they had come to entertain the troops.

After the war, the hospital, which had been named Pratt General after pioneering Army flight surgeon Fabian Pratt, was converted to a Veterans Administration facility and used in a cooperative teaching agreement with the nearby University of Miami. The VA operated the facility for more than twenty years, when the agency finally moved to a modern plant near Miami's medical center.

Federal budget officials of the late 1960s saw the abandoned hospital as an enormous white elephant, a building that had outlived its usefulness long ago. The wisdom in Washing-

BELOW: This Coral Gables business, Esslinger-Wooten-Maxwell Realtors, took a modern approach when adopting some of the city's architectural flavor for use in its headquarters building on South Dixie Highway. BOTTOM: The Coral Gables War Memorial Youth Center, which hosts a wide variety of programs for children and adults, was recently remodeled and is now one of the most colorful facilities downtown.

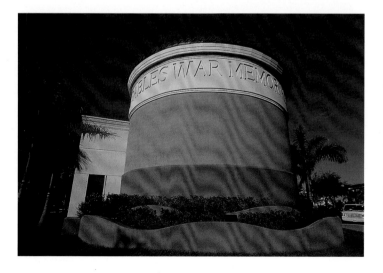

ton was to sell. Given the property's prime location, there were plenty of developers eager to demolish the structure and begin parceling out the building lots.

At another time, or in another place, it might have happened. But by the end of the 1960s, public awareness of architectural legacies had been heightened in Coral Gables, and "Save the Biltmore" was to become a rallying cry in the city's history.

In 1971, voters passed a $3 million bond issue intended for the purchase of the property from the government. In the meantime, however, momentum had grown in the U.S. Congress for Richard Nixon's Legacy of Parks Program and the Historic Monument Act, designed to protect such historic treasures as the Biltmore from the wrecker's ball. The legislation was passed in 1972, and the property was granted back to the city in 1973, with Julie Nixon Eisenhower presenting the deed to Mayor Keith Phillips Jr.

The city had its grand hotel back, at last, but it was essentially a ruin, its former grandeur little more than a memory. Estimates for its massive restoration began at $8 million, but insiders scoffed, insisting that price would not begin to cover the costs necessary for its repairs.

The city began to cast about for deep-pocket (CONTINUED ON PAGE 155)

Preservation as a Way of Life

In November 1992, Florida voters passed by a huge margin an amendment to the state constitution allowing a county or municipality to grant tax exemptions to encourage owners of historically significant properties to rehabilitate those holdings in accordance with preservationist guidelines. In March of the following year, Dade County (as it was called then) became the first in the state to adopt an ordinance allowing for waiver of county taxes for such purposes. In May, Coral Gables enacted its own ordinance, freezing taxes at pre-improvement rates for a period of ten years for owners agreeing to observe carefully drawn guidelines. It was a grassroots movement for those committed to preservation of the many treasured landmarks in Coral Gables, but hardly the first.

The community had been sensitized to the issues of historic preservation since the late 1960s, when the threat of demolition hovered over both the massive Douglas Entrance and the venerable Biltmore Hotel. Efforts by local government and concerned citizens saved both structures and led to the establishment of the Coral Gables Historic Preservation Board in 1973, along with the passage of the first local historical preservation ordinance in Dade County.

In 1984, the city established the position of Historic Landmark Officer, and by 1986, the city's continuing efforts had garnered certification from the National Park Service, allowing it to compete for national grant funding and to provide local evaluation and input on buildings nominated for inclusion on the National Register of Historic Places.

In 1994, the Office of Historic Preservation became an official department of Coral Gables city government, a virtually unheard-of development in civic governance, where such bodies are normally accorded an advisory capacity at most. "It just seemed natural to me," says Ellen Uguccioni, who became Historic Landmark Officer in 1985. "Because preservation touches so many areas of the Coral Gables community, it was only appropriate that we be equal in status with other city departments."

Uguccioni, who assumed the position of Historic Preservation Administrator in 1990 and still heads the Historic Preservation Department for the city, points with pride to the early planning and the rich quality of life that most would agree has derived from those first decisions. "It is amazing how much continuity has been maintained," she says, "but it is equally important to continue and expand what we do. In Coral Gables, planning and preservation really define what our community is."

Ellen Uguccioni, the city's director of historic preservation since 1985, one of the few such positions in the country for a city this size.

The Biltmore Hotel has remained a visual exclamation point for Coral Gables since the 1920s. Through the years, the Biltmore has maintained its reputation as one of the world's most striking hotels.

Scenes—from modern-day to founding days—of the University of Miami. BELOW: Recent additions to the campus have taken on a regional flair. BOTTOM RIGHT: The campus lake as it appeared in the 1950s. TOP RIGHT: The student center as it appeared on a postcard in the 1950s; this building has since been replaced.

developers with a sense of historical obligation, but it wasn't an easy task. The anomalous location, miles from those sparkling Florida beaches, still plagued the prospect in the eyes of many.

The city did what it could. Part of a $7 million federal grant was used to renovate the Country Club building for use as a restaurant and art museum, but it was a short-lived operation. Then, in 1985, an agreement was finally reached with a development team that would spend nearly $50 million to restore the Biltmore.

In just over a year, not much more than the time it took to build the hotel in the first place, the rehabilitation was complete and the Biltmore Hotel once again opened its doors.

For those who had seen the state to which the building had descended, this rise from the ashes was nothing short of amazing. Bands back in the ballroom, chefs returned to the kitchens, state-of-the-art clubhouses for tennis players and golfers, not to mention new courts and a refurbished golf course. It all seemed too good to be true . . . and suddenly, it seemed that it was.

In late 1990, the development group that owned the hotel went into receivership, and the hotel, heartbreakingly, was closed once again. Those who had come to love the old building had begun to wonder just what past sins were being punished in such cruel fashion.

This time the windows would stay dark for two years before new management came on the scene. In August 1992, the Seaway Hotels Corporation reopened the Biltmore and has operated it since, its resurgence a symbol of the city's historical sig-

nificance and its commitment to the preservation of the enduring values of graciousness, hospitality, and style.

The Biltmore is not the only great Coral Gables institution to endure and prosper, of course. Were he still alive to see it, George Merrick would surely point to a site just a mile or so to the southeast of the grand old hotel where the greatest of his legacies is to be found.

From the earliest days of Miami's development, civic leaders had discussed the need for a university to serve as a nexus for the emerging community's educational and cultural aspirations. In 1916, William Jennings Bryan crystallized these vague notions in a plan for a school that would draw students from all the Americas—"The Pan-American University," he called it.

Still, it was not until George Merrick entered the picture in 1925 that plans for a South Florida university became a reality.

In 1925, Merrick donated 160 prime acres of Coral Gables property and $5 million of his own money in order to found the University of Miami, "destined to become the cultural center of the entire South." Five million dollars in matching pledges were secured from other area philanthropists, and local attorney William E. Walsh, Frederic Zeigen, and Merrick obtained a charter for the University from Dade County. The University's original Board of Regents included Merrick, Bryan, Clayton Cooper of the *Miami Tribune,* James M. Cox of the *Miami News,* Mitchell Price, president of the Dade County Bar, and various other prominent community members.

The cornerstone for the Solomon G. Merrick Building, the first on the main campus, was laid on

Lake Osceola at the University of Miami. The path around the lake provides perfect scenery for joggers or students going to class. There are many fish, turtles, and birds living in and around the lake, which is often rumored to also contain an alligator or two. Manatees are sometimes spotted in the canals flowing from this lake.

February 4, 1926, and was the occasion for Merrick's heartfelt declaration that the undertaking marked the pinnacle of his aspirations for the new community ("I pledge now and through the years the best that is in me to its upbuilding . . . "). Construction moved forward with characteristic Merrick alacrity on the fanciful Paist/Fink-designed project, intended to house the University's administration. Archival photographs show that the superstructure for the building had taken on its essential shape when the hurricane blasted through on September 18.

While such a disaster might have understandably daunted other administrators, Bowman Foster Ashe, school secretary and later its first president, was determined that the University would open its doors. Though there is some debate whether it was the damage done by the hurricane or the failure of the matching pledges to materialize that led to the abandonment of the

unfinished Merrick building, there is no question about what happened next. Carpenters were hastily dispatched to partition the larger rooms in the yet-unfinished Anastasia Hotel with plasterboard so that a sufficient number of classrooms could be made available, and the nearby San Sebastian was pressed into service as a dormitory for students.

On October 15, less than a month after the hurricane, a few hundred students and their faculty,

LEFT: The Orange Bowl started as a small game on New Year's Day in 1933, with the school being one of the participants. Though the original University plan included a stadium in the Gables, it was eventually decided to move the game closer to downtown Miami. Nonetheless, the Hurricane football team (above right) later became a national powerhouse.

all singing "Yes, We Are Collegiate," marched into the first classes held at what was to be dubbed the "Cardboard College." A week later, the University fielded its first football team, an all-freshman club that overcame Rollins College and went undefeated at 8-0.

While Merrick and others may have been heartened by this steadfast effort to establish higher education's presence in Coral Gables, it is doubtful they could have foreseen all of the struggles that lay ahead. With the ensuing collapse of the local and national economies, college became a luxury afforded only a very few. In more than one instance, President Ashe was reduced to borrowing on his personal insurance policy in order to meet the faculty payroll. By 1932, the University had collapsed into bankruptcy, and on August 7 of that year, Ashe was to form a new University of Miami Corporation, which purchased the entirety of the University's property at auction with a bid of $15,758.84.

Despite financial woes that would plague it well into the last half of the century, the University had forged ahead with the development of its mission. A student newspaper, the *University News*, had been established, and was later aptly renamed the *Miami Hurricane*. In 1928, the School of Law was formally recognized by the Florida Supreme Court. A campus radio station began broadcasts in 1930, and by 1932, an eight-thousand-volume library had been established, with Dorothy Miller hired as the first full-time librarian.

The University of Miami also would figure in the establishment of another fixture of the South Florida scene during its early days. Shortly after the school's reorganization, local boosters approached Henry Doherty, then owner of the Biltmore Hotel, with a request that he bankroll a New Year's Day football game. Doherty agreed, contributing $3,000 to ensure the 1933 match, which just a few years later would become the Orange Festival, with the Orange Bowl Football Classic as its main event.

While the Orange Festival may have flourished, the University itself struggled through the depression years. During World War II, the University became a major training center for U.S. and allied aviators, not only providing an influx of much-needed cash at the time, but also preparing a new crop of students who would long to return to the balmy site of their wartime instruction.

In 1947, the University added its School of Engineering and began the excavation of Lake Osceola, the original reflecting pool envisioned by Merrick. The Memorial Classroom Building, designed by Robert Law Weed and Marion Manley, the first registered woman architect in Florida, was also completed in 1947 and is today the main classroom building. A Student Club, praised by architectural critics for its integration with the tropical environment, was completed in 1948. And in 1949, the Solomon Merrick Building, which had remained a skeletal reminder of better intentions for twenty-three years, was at last completed (though its original Mediterranean design had been discarded).

Soldiers returning on the G. I. Bill doubled, then tripled, the school's enrollment. In 1952, the year that also marked the death of President Bowman Ashe, the School of Medicine opened at Pratt General Hospital, thereby melding the destinies of two

of George Merrick's most ambitious dreams, if only for a few years.

The institution's development over the last half of the century has transformed it far beyond its founders' expectations. A series of gifts and purchases has extended Merrick's original 160 acres to nearly 260 acres today. The primary teaching facility for the School of Medicine is now located at Jackson Memorial Medical Center, a sixty-seven-

An admirer takes a moment to mimic the life-like mask art at the sprawling Beaux Arts Festival on the University of Miami campus, held annually in January.

acre complex, including Jackson Memorial Hospital, just west of downtown Miami. Such a relationship with a major public hospital is unique in the United States and likely contributes to the medical school's perennial ranking among the best in the country. Significant advances in Alzheimer's disease, spinal cord injury and paralysis, diabetes, cancer, ophthalmology, and AIDS have been made by researchers at the School of Medicine.

The University of Miami has grown to become the largest private research university in the southeastern United States, with a faculty of nearly two thousand, 94 percent of whom hold the Ph.D. or terminal degree in their field. There are some 14,000 students enrolled today, nearly half of those in 160 graduate and professional programs. The National Science Foundation ranks the University thirty-seventh among universities overall

and sixteenth among private universities in expenditures of federal research funds.

The School of Business, founded just three years after the University opened, has grown into the second largest school on the Coral Gables campus. More importantly to the city of Coral Gables, the school—which offers a full complement of undergraduate, graduate, and doctoral degree programs, including one of the largest Executive M.B.A. programs in the nation—has educated many of the area's business leaders and has become a valuable resource to the local corporate community.

As the stature and size of Coral Gables grew, so did that of the business school. In recent years, the school has brought to campus such notable speakers as H. Ross Perot; Alvah H. Chapman Jr.; David H. Komansky; Roberto C. Goizueta; and Charles E. Rice. The 1980 dedication of the George W. Jenkins Building, named for the founder of Publix Supermarkets, meant that,

BELOW: With some 14,000 students and 262 undergraduate, graduate, doctoral, and professional programs, the University of Miami is large enough to encompass virtually every intellectual discipline, yet small enough to be of human scale for its students.

for the first time in its history, the school had a permanent home.

The home was expanded in 1997 with a forty-eight-thousand-square-foot addition. The new three hundred-seat Storer Auditorium was made possible through School of Business alumni Peter and Virginia Storer and the generous support of the George B. Storer Foundation. The James W. McLamore Executive Education Center is named for the late co-founder of Burger King and former chairman of the University of Miami Board of Trustees. The creation of the McLamore Center marks the beginning of an important phase in the school's involvement in non-degree executive education.

The Rosenstiel School of Marine and Atmospheric Science, established in 1943, now ranks among the top marine research institutes in the world. Where once it was impossible to find the $5 million to match Merrick's original pledge, a five-year fund-raising effort that concluded in 1989

The University of Miami is the largest private research university in the southeastern United States. The National Science Foundation ranks the University thirty-seventh among all universities and sixteenth among private universities in expenditures of federal research and development funds.

totaled $517 million, and gifts from alumni, friends, and organizations for 1997 alone amounted to nearly $80 million.

There have been any number of milestones along the way, of course: many residents still recall Dr. Martin Luther King's stirring lecture on the campus in 1966, and faculty point with pride to the day in 1982 when the University's election to membership in Phi Beta Kappa was announced.

The University's sports programs have provided many thrills for the entire South Florida community as well. In 1982, the baseball team confirmed its status as one of the premier programs in the country by winning its first of two national championships (the other came in 1985) in the College World Series. In 1984, the Hurricane football team began what is often referred to as the "decade of dominance" in that sport, winning its first national championship. Three more championship teams in football were to follow in 1987, 1989, and 1991.

In 1986, the University celebrated its sixtieth anniversary by being named among the nine best "young universities" in the nation. Today, the University's president—only its fourth in more than seventy years—is Edward T. Foote II, former journalist and attorney, and one-time dean of the Washington University School of Law. It was Foote who headed the major fund-raising efforts of the 1980s and 1990s and elevated the endowment to $310 million. Under his leadership, the University of Miami has added more than three hundred new faculty positions and has dramatically increased the quality of entering students: more than two-thirds of entering freshmen are in the top fifth of their high school ranks. With more than seventy-five hundred full-time employees and an annual budget of some $800 million, the institution has become the second largest private employer in Miami-Dade County: a formidable record of achievement indeed for an institution founded in the midst of natural and

The University of Miami School of Business offers a full complement of undergraduate, graduate, and doctoral degree programs, including one of the largest Executive M.B.A. programs in the country. In 1997 the school opened the Storer Auditorium and the James W. McLamore Executive Education Center. The creation of the McLamore Center marks the beginning of an important new phase in the school's involvement in non-degree executive education.

164

financial disaster. But all the facts and figures, the academic excellence, the athletic trophies, and the individual achievements pale beside the greater intangible benefits that Merrick sensed lay in store. As he put it during his address at the groundbreaking ceremony back in 1926: "Hotels, clubs, all the great material things that Miami had accomplished, beautiful, wonderful, glorious though they may be, are but ephemeral insignificance beside this great enterprise of permanently

real and vital influence upon the lives and hearts of present and future Miami . . . ."

The changes reflected in the University of Miami's development over the last half of the twentieth century mirror in many ways the progress of the city itself. The 1930s constituted a period of doldrums for Coral Gables as a whole. Those fifty-six hundred residents in 1930 came to know each other fairly well over the decade lead-

employed by the Works Progress Administration, the first project of that agency to be completed in the city. Another Phineas Paist design, uncharacteristic in its classic simplicity, was built in 1941: the First Church of Christ Scientist.

But for the most part, the look of the city remained the same. Most of the original Dade County pines, a particularly dense and sap-rich variant of the Southern pine that had covered the landscape from the beginning of the city's development, were gone, victims of the 1926 hurricane. The luxuriant trees that hadn't been snapped like twigs by the big winds had died soon after of storm-related stress and beetle infestation (much as the vast pine canopy of South Dade was virtually destroyed by Hurricane Andrew in 1992).

Merrick's foresight in importing all those exotic plants had paid off, however. Banyan, ficus, palm, hibiscus, oleander, and other vegetation would thrive, unaffected by the economic woes of the depression. Wartime recruits who were brought to South Florida for training—men who had never seen a palm tree, encountered a winter-flowering shrub or felt the caress of a tropical breeze—would carry memories of such delights with them for years. Given the war's ending and a booming resurgence in the economy, it is no surprise that so many of those trainees would choose to return.

The population of Coral Gables, stagnant for so long, nearly doubled in 1945, and doubled again by 1950, when there were nearly twenty thousand residents. By 1955, the population had neared thirty thousand, and by 1960, following the vast

(CONTINUED ON PAGE 169)

ing up to World War II, and the appearance of the city remained much as it had been when the Coral Gables Corporation failed in 1929.

A few structures of note were completed after the "golden age" of building in the city: The First Methodist Church on Coral Way, designed by Phineas Paist and Harold Steward, was constructed in 1933. The Coral Gables Woman's Club, which also came to house an expanded city library for a time, was completed in 1937 by workers

Chamber of Chambers

While George Merrick's original plans for Coral Gables included a concerted effort to encourage retail and commercial development in his new city, he also understood that the chief impetus for such growth would come from merchants and businessmen themselves. On August 4, 1925, barely three months following the incorporation of the city, the Coral Gables Chamber of Commerce was chartered, with six local businessmen as signatories.

From that modest beginning, the Chamber has grown to a membership of more than sixteen hundred business and professional firms working together to encourage development; guide future growth in a fashion consistent with Gables tradition, interests, and ideals; and assist in making the city the best possible place to live and work. The Chamber's mission statement reads: "To foster and enhance the economic interests and quality of life in the Coral Gables community."

One recent manifestation of these endeavors has been the formation and spinoff of the Coral Gables Business Improvement District, whereby downtown business owners agreed to a special tax aimed at revitalizing the area and enriching its cultural life through an integrated program of capital improvement, sponsorship of special events, and implementation of code changes including those affecting parking relaxation, sidewalk cafes, valet parking, and the like.

Chamber President Ron Robison, himself a city commissioner from 1982 to 1985, and one of the authors of the Mediterranean Design ordinance, points with pride to these and other such activities. "We have just 6 percent of our land used for commercial purposes, but our tax base is about fifty-fifty residential/downtown-commercial," he says. "That balance is what allows us to maintain our outstanding quality of life. We just work to make sure that our growth is in keeping with the original vision of Coral Gables as a one-of-a-kind place to be."

In recognition of such efforts, the Florida Chamber of Commerce Executives named the Gables Chamber the 1997 Chamber of Commerce of the Year.

FAR LEFT: The Coral Gables Chamber of Commerce, on the impetus of George Merrick, was one of the city's first chartered organizations, established in 1925. LEFT: A Bicentennial time capsule buried in 1976 still has a few generations to go before being unearthed.

post-revolution exodus from Cuba, another five thousand had come to call the Gables home. By 1970, the population had exceeded forty thousand, the level where it has remained since. (There is a very simple reason for that plateau by the way, on which Merrick's nephew Donald Kuhn sheds

light. Asked during a recent visit to comment on the biggest change he saw in the city between the era of his childhood and the present day, Kuhn responded quickly: "No more vacant lots.")

Much of what has been built upon those no-longer vacant lots has diverged considerably from

Though not in Coral Gables, Baptist Hospital has distinct architectural ties to the city. Its principal architect was Harold D. Steward, who was a partner with Phineas Paist, perhaps the most important architect in determining the look of the Gables. The hospital's corporate parent, Baptist Health Systems of South Florida, relocated its headquarters to Coral Gables in 1998.

the original Merrick style, of course: changing tastes and escalating costs led to the abandonment of the Mediterranean Revival approach in both public and private construction, a shift that is nowhere more noticeable than the contrast seen north and south of U.S. 1. Magnificent homes abound in both sections, of course, but a drive from the north city boundary to the southern boundary, while taking only a half-hour in real time, spans about seventy-five years in architectural history; and once that boundary is crossed, there is little to see as a reminder of Merrick's original vision.

Something more than taste is involved as well, a lesson that was brought home during the struggle over the future of the Biltmore property. While progress and a fascination with the new have been a part of the American experience from the first days of the republic, a comprehensive view of history and cultural development reminds us of the importance of maintaining a connection with heritage. Growth and change informed by practices and values proved sound and nurturing by experiences of the past is a mode of development with which most reasonable citizens would concur, in theory at least. Balanced against this understanding is the desire of every generation to seek its own identity, manifesting its interests and its ideals not only in customs, laws, and cultural amenities, but in its public and private building as well.

Understandable perhaps that a generation so beaten down by the Great Depression, so wearied by the vast struggle of World War II, and so buoyed by that ultimate triumph, should return

ABOVE: HealthSouth Doctors' Hospital has found a strong niche in outdoor oriented Coral Gables—it is the premier sports-medicine provider in the area. It also has a strong neuroscience program. BELOW: Sevilla Center on Sevilla Avenue offers up an interesting contrast of sharp angles and soft curves.

to "normal" life firmly fixed upon the notion of "Out with the old, in with the new." Moreover, practicality alone might argue against the expenditure of $48 million to restore an old hotel that could conceivably struggle forever to provide a return on such an investment.

Just as clearly, though, there is something more important to so many than can be provided by practicality and novelty alone. It is an awareness of this fact, prompted in the instance of Coral Gables, no doubt, by the sheer number and ubiquity of the city's historic structures, that explains why citizens would band together in sufficient number not only to lift an ancient hotel from the grave of neglect but to enact ordinances that ensure the preservation of such legacies forever.

In 1973, concurrent with a growing public awareness and passage of na-

tional preservation legislation (and shortly after the success of saving the Douglas Entrance and the Biltmore Hotel from the wrecker's ball), the city of Coral Gables adopted its first Historic Preservation ordinance, designed among other things to identify, evaluate, record, protect, restore, and rebuild properties deemed significant to the history and culture of the community. The measure (the first of its kind in Dade County) was revised and expanded in 1984, when the Historic Preservation Board was created. It was amended again in 1990 when the process for adding buildings to the National Register of Historic Places was clarified.

A Historic Preservation Department is responsible for identifying significant properties and for reviewing planned modifications and alterations to properties on that list. In addition, the office

BELOW: The faces in stone relief on the original Police and Fire Station have always been eyecatching in their real-life expressions. RIGHT: Coral Gables City Hall.

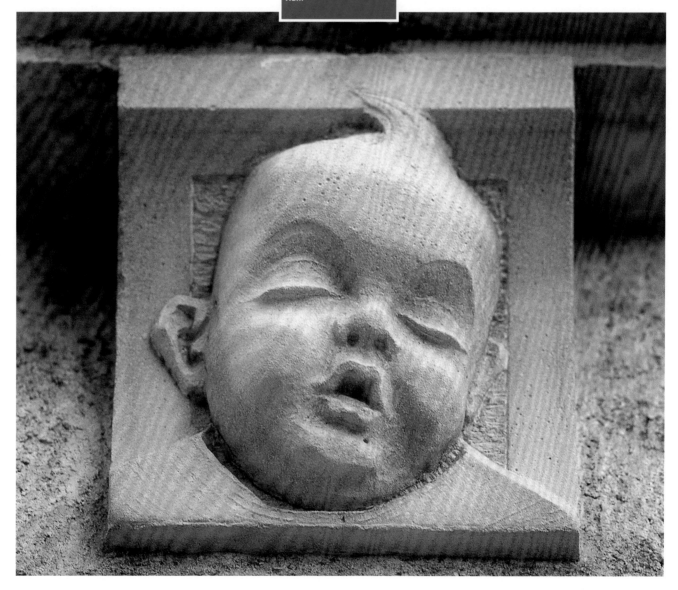

CITY HALL
OF
CORAL GABLES
1927

COMMISSIONERS

EDWARD E. DAMMERS
MAYOR

GEORGE E. MERRICK
DON PEABODY
E. T. PVRCELL
F. W. WEBSTER

R. M. DAVIDSON
CITY MANAGER

and its director are active in seeking state and federal funds to support local preservation projects, and in the education of the community as regards the benefits of historical preservation.

An important feature of the program is the inclusion of certain tax incentives: owners of properties listed in either the National or the Coral Gables Register of Historic Places, who meet specific improvement standards, are eligible to have their property taxes frozen for up to ten years at the rate paid prior to improvement. Because of the stability provided by such legislation and the attention drawn to the unique character of buildings added to the historic rolls, owners who have participated in the program have traditionally seen their property values rise. While historic designation comes as a result of public hearing and deliberation, properties generally must be at least fifty years old and have significant association with historical event, personage, or architectural design.

To date, more than seventy-five properties, including private homes, schools, churches, shops, and offices, have been listed on the Coral Gables Register. Many are in the National Register as well, including the original Coral Gables Merrick House on Coral Way, the Biltmore Hotel and Country Club, Venetian Pool, Coral Gables

ABOVE: Coral Gables has become such a haven as the North American corporate headquarters for Central and South American companies that local bookstores keep a ready supply of newspapers from the home countries. RIGHT AND BELOW: Bill's Pipe and Tobacco Shop, though no longer owned by Bill Taub, has nonetheless been a downtown fixture for over twenty-five years on Ponce de Leon Boulevard. Over 80 percent of the cigars come from the Dominican Republic and Honduras.

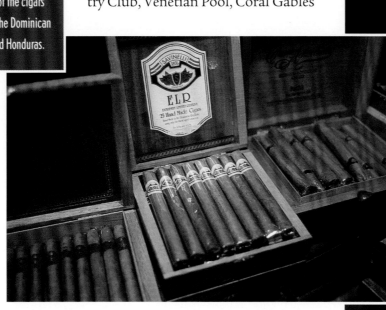

City Hall, the Congregational Church, the Douglas Entrance and more.

In addition to preservation activities, a Mediterranean Architectural Ordinance adopted in 1986 provides incentives to developers building or renovating any building in the Mediterranean style. To offset the higher costs of employing that style, the City grants development bonuses and special allowances in regard to building height, parking requirements, usable square footage and the like. As a result, most commercial development under-

taken in the last decade has incorporated many of the stylistic touches characteristic of the city's oldest structures.

One of the more significant benefits of the creation and maintenance of such a setting has been its attractiveness for corporate interests looking to position themselves advantageously for Latin American or other regional operations. In 1951, Standard Oil of New Jersey (still doing business in Coral Gables as Esso Inter-America, with 130 employees) became the first major corporation to

177

The Hyatt Regency Coral Gables Hotel located at 50 Alhambra Plaza is just one of several top-quality hotels located in the city. The Regency was built in 1988 and has 242 rooms.

move its headquarters to Coral Gables. While such relocations continued steadily afterwards, it was in 1966, when Dow Chemical Corporation came to the Gables after a much-ballyhooed international search, that things really took off. Later, in 1977, an article in the *Harvard Business Review* predicted that Coral Gables would become "one of the three global cities of the future" because of its strategic location.

By the mid-1990s, nearly 150 multinational corporations had established Latin American or other regional headquarters in Coral Gables: Alcoa, Texaco, Seagram, Rockwell International, American Airlines, Delta Air Lines, Hilton International, Nabisco, Ralston Purina, Disney Consumer Products, E. I. duPont, Del Monte, and many more. Eventually 55 percent of Dow's revenue would come from operations outside the United States, leading Yves Bobillier, president of Dow Chemical Latin America, to assert that the decision to locate in Coral Gables had played a key role in that success.

"Coral Gables reminds me in many ways of Hong Kong, Geneva, and New York," the Swiss-born Bobillier said, "places that have parlayed their diverse ethnicities and languages to become world-class centers of international business and finance."

In addition to the multinational corporate pres-

ence in Coral Gables, there are twenty-one countries with consular, foreign trade, or tourism offices in the city, including Denmark, Thailand, Great Britain, Hungary, Mexico, Spain, and Taiwan. Thirty-two domestic banking institutions have offices in the city, along with forty-two foreign bank agencies and eleven Edge Act banks authorized solely for the conduct of international transactions.

Further evidence of the strength of the city's economic base is seen in the fact that while less than five percent of the city's land is devoted to commercial use, this same property provides nearly half of the tax revenues. And while the perception may be that citizens of Coral Gables are taxed heavily in order to maintain the "Gables standard," the fact is that millage rates are ranked twenty-sixth among the twenty-nine governmental agencies in Miami-Dade County (the county name change came in 1997).

The city itself is governed by a City Commission/City Manager arrangement, with three commissioners and a mayor (at the time of this writing, the latter position was held by Raul J. Valdes-Fauli, the first Hispanic mayor in the city's history and in his third term). There are 840 city employees and an annual budget that has grown to more than $70 million.

(CONTINUED ON PAGE 180)

Gateway to the Americas

In 1927, King Alfonso XIII of Spain signed a decoration for George Merrick, "in appreciation of the recognition you have given Spanish architecture in the building of the City of Coral Gables." The decoration arrived in South Florida along with a gift of a seventeenth-century trunk and an armoire from the same period, still on display at The Merrick House. For the first forty years of Coral Gables's existence, the gifts and the proclamation from the King of Spain constituted most of the actual interchange between the new community and the culture from which much of its architecture, its street names, and its essential ambience had been derived.

All that was to change in the latter half of the twentieth century, however: The Cuban Revolution of 1959 resulted in a great influx of Hispanic residents to Coral Gables. Successive waves of immigration from Cuba and elsewhere in Central and South America have added more, until today 46.5 percent of the city's forty-three thousand residents are of Hispanic descent, with 35 percent having been born outside the United States.

Since 1972, Spain has maintained the offices and residence of a General Consulate in Coral Gables. There are also Spanish Trade Commission offices, a Spanish-American Chamber of Commerce, and an office of tourism, along with similar official representation from Colombia, Ecuador, Guatemala, Mexico, Uruguay, Honduras, and many more Latin American countries, as well as Puerto Rico.

In 1993, Raul J. Valdes-Fauli became the first Hispanic mayor of Coral Gables. At the time of this writing, he was serving his third consecutive two-year term, tying the record of former Mayor George Corrigan. Valdes-Fauli, who was born in Cuba in 1943 and who received a law degree from Harvard, came to the United States in 1961 and has lived in Coral Gables since the 1970s.

"We are indeed a multicultural, multiethnic, multinational community," Valdes-Fauli says. "We have become the business center for U.S. companies with significant operations in Latin America, and with our several dozen art galleries, we are neck and neck with Mexico City as the contemporary art center of the Americas.

"All the excitement and richness of living in Coral Gables derives from being outward looking," he adds. "We honor the past, but we're not anchored in it. We take advantage of the prevailing winds of change."

ABOVE: An actress applies make-up before going on stage. TOP RIGHT: Actors' Playhouse at the Miracle Theatre's Artistic Director David Arisco, Executive Director Barbara Stein, and Foundation Chairman Lawrence Stein, DDS. BOTTOM RIGHT: Shown is a musical number from the Actors' Playhouse critically acclaimed *West Side Story* performed in fall 1997.

Without question, Coral Gables has become Miami-Dade County's most desirable residential community: the median house value is nearly three hundred thousand dollars, and more than half of its fourteen square miles are devoted to single-family residences, with another 30 percent set aside for recreational and public use. Less than 1 percent of the area is devoted to industrial use. In addition to the cultural activities provided by the University of Miami, which houses the collections of the Lowe Art Museum, the city harbors more than twenty-five private art galleries, two major bookstores, and several acting companies, including the Actors' Playhouse at the Miracle Theatre, on its namesake street, adorned with its historic signature art deco design. In addition, the city is home to the New Theatre, Florida Shakespeare Theatre, Teatro Avante, and the International Hispanic Theatre Festival. In music are the Coral Gables Chamber Symphony and Opera, the Miami Symphony Orchestra, and the Mainly Mozart Festival.

The city is well known as the restaurant capital of South Florida, with more than 120 establishments representing every cuisine the world

around—not the least among them Florida nouveau—with many restaurants winning national and international acclaim. Not content to rest on their laurels, downtown businessmen and civic leaders have pushed for a number of recent changes in city codes to increase the number of sidewalk cafes and allow for more outdoor events of a cultural nature, thereby adding to the European flair of an evening stroll through the commercial district.

The years of Coral Gables's growth have not always been placid, of course. In some ways it is a miracle that the city survived the blows of those early years; that it not only survived but has pros-

pered, with much of its original glamour and raison d'être intact, is a testament to the vision of its founder.

A 1997 local newspaper editorial posed again the question of whether George E. Merrick had been overmemorialized in the city. This is a curious question, to be sure. There is a short George E. Merrick Street on the University of Miami campus—an apt honor, no doubt, but there are many grander boulevards in Miami-Dade County bearing the names of those who have given far less to the community, including more than one among them bearing the name of a convicted felon. There is a brief spur called Merrick Way, linking Miracle

Mile with Alhambra Plaza, and of course there is picturesque Merrick Park, a small patch of greensward that sits just south of City Hall, where a clerk or an office worker can enjoy lunch in the shade, and where, in season, the annual holiday display draws thousands of children and parents to stroll among the glittering lights and decorated trees. There is also the Merrick Building on the University of Miami campus, but that structure is in fact dedicated to the memory of Solomon Merrick. The Merrick House has been preserved in its original location on Coral Way, but it was a structure built by the family itself, after all. The city has

given the new parking garage the designation of Merrick Place, and there is an annual Merrick Festival and Merrick Dream Ball.

But in all of Coral Gables, there is no plaza, fountain, entrance, grand public building, nor bronze statue that honors Merrick. Overmemorialized? Hardly, though it is doubtful George Merrick would complain. If there is a vantage point from which he might gaze down upon what his beloved city has become, he would likely wave his hand and invite everyone to behold as great a memorial he could ever have envisioned: Coral Gables, we call it, the City Beautiful.

FAR LEFT: The striking colors of downtown Coral Gables are always evident. ABOVE: Cafe Demetrio opened in early 1998, featuring special coffees and an outdoor patio. LEFT: The lunch crowd at La Palma enjoy dining outdoors, even in February, when this shot was taken in 1998.

George Merrick, who loved grand entrances, would have been proud of this, built recently—and decorated for the holidays—at Douglas Road and Miracle Mile.

CORAL GABLES

Properties Within the City of Coral Gables Listed in the National Register of Historic Places

Biltmore Hotel
1200 Anastasia Avenue
Date Listed: 9/22/72
(Listed as a National Historic Landmark)

Coral Gables Woman's Club
1001 East Ponce de Leon Boulevard
Date Listed: 3/27/90

City Hall—City of Coral Gables
405 Biltmore Way
Date Listed: 7/24/74

Douglas Entrance
800 Douglas Entrance
Date Listed: 9/22/72

Coral Gables Congregational Church
3010 DeSoto Boulevard
Date Listed: 10/10/78

MacFarlane Homestead Subdivision
Historic District
Date Listed: 5/26/94

Coral Gables Merrick House
907 Coral Way
Date Listed: 4/13/73

Old Police and Fire Station
285 Aragon Avenue
Date Listed: 11/6/84

Coral Gables Elementary School
105 Minorca Avenue
Date Listed: 6/30/88

Venetian Pool and Casino
2701 De Soto Boulevard
Date Listed: 8/20/81

Coral Gables Register of Historic Landmarks

Alhambra Plaza
Alhambra Plaza Street Median and Historic Roadway
Designer: Denman Fink
Date Enacted: 8/30/88

Alhambra Water Tower
Water Tower Intersection at Alhambra Circle, Greenway Court
and Ferdinand Street
Designer: Denman Fink
Date Enacted: 11/8/88

Apartment at 3110 Segovia Street
Architect: Charles Paul Nieder
Date Enacted: 11/9/93

Arts Center Building
Office Building at 2901 Ponce de Leon Boulevard
Architect: Phineas Paist
Date Enacted: 2/24/87

Balboa Plaza
Coral Way, Intersection at South Greenway Drive, De Soto
Boulevard, and Anderson Road
Designer: Denman Fink
Date Enacted: 8/30/88

Bennett Building
Mixed Apartment / Retail
713 Biltmore Way
Architect: H. George Fink
Date Enacted: 3/22/83

Boy Scout Troop #7 (Fireplace and Chimney)
South Side of Granada Golf Course, between Cordova Street
and Columbus Boulevard
Architect Phineas Paist
Date Enacted: 8/17/93

Briggs/Haddock House
Residence at 920 Coral Way
Architect: H. George Fink
Date Enacted: 10/10/78

Cla-Reina / La Palma Hotel
Hotel Apartments at 116 Alhambra Circle
Architect: H. George Fink
Date Enacted: 2/24/87

Cocoplum Woman's Club
1375 Sunset Road
Social / Institutional Building
Architects: R. G. Howard and E. A. Early
Dated Enacted: 8/30/88

Colonnade Building / Florida National Bank
Commercial at 169 Miracle Mile
Architects: Phineas Paist, Walter DeGarmo, and Paul Chalfin
and Associates
Date Enacted: 3/12/85

Columbus Plaza
Coral Way, Intersection of Coral Way, Columbus Boulevard,
and Indian Mound Trail
Designer: Denman Fink
Date Enacted: 8/30/88

Commercial Building—Stow Building
270 Alhambra Circle
Architect: H. George Fink
Date Enacted: 3/11/97

Commercial Building at 1569 Sunset Drive
Architect: Martin Hauri
Date Enacted: 3/8/94

Commercial Entrance
Intersection Alhambra Circle, Madeira Avenue, and
Douglas Road
Designer: Denman Fink
Date Enacted: 8/30/88

Coral Gables City Hall
Government Building
405 Biltmore Way
Architects: Phineas Paist and Denman Fink
Date Enacted: 2/26/85

Coral Gables Congregation Church
3010 De Soto Boulevard
Architects: Kiehnel and Elliott
Date Enacted: 7/25/89

Coral Gables Elementary School
School at 105 Minorca Avenue
Architects: Kiehnel and Elliott
Date Enacted: 4/30/85

Coral Gables House
907 Coral Way
Date Enacted: 4/30/85

Coral Gables Woman's Club
1001 Ponce de Leon Boulevard
Social Institutional Club
Works Project Administration (W.P.A.)
Date Enacted: 4/26/77

Coral Way (SW 24th Street) Roadway
That portion of Coral Way lying between Le Jeune Road on the
East, and Red Road on the West
Date Enacted: 3/23/76

Country Club Prado Entrance
Country Club Prado and SW 8th Street
Designer: Denman Fink
Date Enacted: 9/29/87

Dammers / Emkjer House
Residence at 1141 Coral Way
Architect: H. George Fink
Date Enacted: 10/10/78

Denman Fink Residence
760 Anastasia Avenue
Architect: Marion Manley
Date Enacted: 10/11/94

De Soto Plaza and Fountain
Intersection at Sevilla Avenue, Granada Boulevard, and
De Soto Boulevard
Designer: Denman Fink
Date Enacted: 8/30/88

Doctor McShane Residence
1253 Anastasia Avenue
Architect: Carl Apuzzo
Date Enacted: 10/8/91

Douglas Entrance / "La Puerta del Sol"
800 Douglas Entrance
Architects: Walter DeGarmo, Phineas Paist, and Denman Fink
Date Enacted: 4/30/85

Douglas / Trager House
Residence at 36 Phonetia Avenue
Architect: H. George Fink
Date Enacted: 2/26/85

Dutch South African Village
6612, 6700, 6710, 6704 Le Jeune Road
6705 San Vincente Street
Architects: Marion Sims Wyeth
Date Enacted: 10/27/87

Freeland Beckham House
Residence at 4209 Santa Maria Street
Builder: Unknown
Date Enacted: 11/10/81

French Normandy Village Historic District (a.k.a. French
Provincial Village)
400, 408, and 412 Alesio Avenue
3622 Le Jeune Road
400, 401, 404, 405, 408, 409, 412, 413, and 416
Viscaya Avenue
3615 and 3621 Viscaya Court
Architects: John and Coulton Skinner
Date Enacted: 9/29/87

George Washington Carver School
238 Grand Avenue
Architects: Walter DeGarmo and Phineas Paist
Date Enacted: 12/10/91

Girl Scout "Little House"
Social/Institutional Use at 3940 Granada Boulevard
Architect: Upton C. Ewing
Date Enacted: 8/17/93

Granada Entrance
Intersection Granada Boulevard and S.W. 8th Street
Designer: Denman Fink
Date Enacted: 8/30/88

Granada Plaza
Intersection at Granada Boulevard and Alhambra Circle
Designer: Denman Fink
Date Enacted: 8/30/88

Granada Shops / Charade Restaurant
Commercial at 2900 Ponce de Leon Boulevard
Architect: Phineas Paist
Date Enacted: 3/22/83

H. George Fink Offices and Studio
Mixed Commercial and Residential
2506 Ponce de Leon Boulevard
Architect: H. George Fink
Date Enacted: 2/26/85

Hotel Place St. Michel
162 Alcazar Avenue
Designers: Anthony Zink and Arthur W. Coote
Date Enacted: 11/14/95

"Java Head" Residence and adjacent property with pool,
and pool house
Residence at 200 Edgewater Drive
Architect: Robert Fitch Smith
Date Enacted: 4/12/88

188

John and Coulton Skinner Thematic Group
3800 Toledo Street, and
714 San Antonio Avenue
Architects: John and Coulton Skinner
Date Enacted: 5/10/94

John M. Stabile Building ("Books & Books")
Mixed Apartment / Retail
296 Aragon Avenue
Architect: John Davis (Addition 1928)
Date Enacted: 2/26/85

Lang-Adams
Residence at 6810 Maynada Street
Date Enacted: 3/22/77

Le Jeune Plaza
Intersection at Miracle Mile and Le Jeune Road
Designers: Denman Fink and Phineas Paist
Date Enacted: 8/30/88

Lummis House (Demolished 1988)
Residence at 3800 Le Jeune Road
Builder: Unknown
Date Enacted: 1/14/86

MacFarlane Homestead—Subdivision Historic District
Primarily owner built
Date Enacted: 9/12/89

Matheson Hammock Park Historic District
Civilian Conservation Corps under direction of R. C. Ward,
       William Lyman Phillips, and A. D. Barnes
Date Enacted: 6/23/92

Merrick / Cleys House
Residence at 937 Coral Way
Builder: Unknown
Date Enacted: 10/10/78

Merrick / Maidique House
Residence at 832 South Greenway Drive
Architect: H. George Fink
Date Enacted: 4/13/85

Miami Biltmore Hotel and Country Club
Hotel / Landscape Grounds
1200 Anastasia Avenue
Architects: Schultze and Weaver
Date Enacted: 2/26/85

Newkirk House (Demolished 1989)
Residence at 1418 Salzedo Street
Architect: H. George Fink
Date Enacted: 2/11/86

Old Police and Fire Station
285 Aragon Avenue
Government / Public Building
Builder: Phineas Paist (W.P.A.)
Date Enacted: 2/26/85

Parmalee / Dewey House
Residence at 2715 Toledo Street
Architect: E. Dean Parmalee
Date Enacted: 2/26/85

Peacock / Tyson House
Residence at 1498 Sevilla Avenue
Addition 1968
Date Enacted: 2/26/85

Pinewood Cemetery
Sunset and Erwin Roads
Date Enacted: 11/18/86

Ponce de Leon Plaza
Intersection of Coral Way and Granada Boulevard (Ornamental
       markers defining formal plaza)
Designers: Denman Fink and Phineas Paist
Date Enacted: 8/30/88

Reedy Parsons Residence
2723 Country Club Prado
Architect: Walter DeGarmo
Date Enacted: 4/22/86

Residence at 422 Alcazar Avenue
Architect: E. Dean Parmalee
Date Enacted: 5/10/94

Residence at 501 Alhambra Circle
Architect: C. Leroy Kinports
Date Enacted: 11/8/94

Residence at 520 Alhambra Circle
Architect: Lee Wade
Date Enacted: 8/30/94

Residence at 644 Alhambra Circle
Architect: Lewis Brumm
Date Enacted: 2/14/95

Residence at 733 Alhambra Circle
Architect: Unknown
Date Enacted: 10/11/84

Residence at 1235 Alhambra Circle
Architect: Unknown
Date Enacted: 6/9/97

Residence at 1258 Alhambra Circle
Architects: Hampton and Reimert
Date Enacted: 10/11/94

Residence at 1302 Alhambra Circle
Architect: C. Leroy Kinports
Date Enacted: 6/11/96

Residence at 2715 Alhambra Circle
Architect: F. McM. Sawyer
Date Enacted: 12/10/91

Residence at 1024 Almeria Avenue
Architect: H. George Fink
Date Enacted: 10/14/97

Residence at 1017 Asturia Avenue
Architect: Lucien Finzi
Date Enacted: 10/10/95

Residence at 1024 Asturia Avenue
Architect: Walter DeGarmo
Date Enacted: 11/12/96

Residence at 1137 Asturia Avenue
Architect: Walter DeGarmo
Date Enacted: 2/14/95

Residence at 1140 Asturia Avenue
Architect: A. L. Klingbeil
Date Enacted: 6/13/95

Residence at 1246 Asturia Avenue
Architect: Lewis Brumm
Date Enacted: 1/12/93

Residence at 1328 Asturia Avenue
Architect: H. George Fink Sr.
Date Enacted: 1/14/97

Residence at 124 Cadima Avenue
Architect: Henry J. Moloney
Date Enacted: 1/18/94

Residence at 619 Camilo Avenue
Architects: Nordin and Nadel
Date Enacted: 3/14/95

Residence at 925 Castile Plaza
Architect: Lewis D. Brumm
Date Enacted: 2/13/96

Residence at 1101 Castile Avenue
Architect: John H. Sculthorpe
Date Enacted: 10/11/94

Residence at 1335 Castile Avenue
Architect: H. George Fink
Date Enacted: 3/11/97

Residence at 1227 Columbus Boulevard
Architect: H. George Fink
Date Enacted: 10/27/92

Residence at 2301 Columbus Boulevard
Architect: Warren E. Richards Co.
Date Enacted: 11/8/94

Residence at 2508 Columbus Boulevard
Architect: H. George Fink (Attribution)
Date Enacted: 1/18/94

Residence at 2512 Columbus Boulevard
Architect: Walter DeGarmo
Date Enacted: 2/14/95

Residence at 2601 Columbus Boulevard
Architect: Otto L. Risch
Date Enacted: 10/10/95

Residence at 2701 Columbus Boulevard
Architect: Walter DeGarmo
Date Enacted: 11/12/96

Residence at 900 Coral Way
Architect: Frank Wyatt Woods
Date Enacted: 10/11/94

Residence at 1032 Coral Way
Architect: Unknown
Date Enacted: 4/25/89

Residence at 2109 Country Club Prado
Architects: Skinner and Pierson
Date Enacted: 2/9/93

Residence at 2421 Country Club Prado
Architects: Kiehnel and Elliott
Date Enacted: 8/29/95

Residence at 2603 Country Club Prado
Architects: Kiehnel and Elliott
Date Enacted: 11/9/93

Residence at 2616 Boulevard
Architect: Walter DeGarmo
Date Enacted: 12/14/93

Residence at 900 El Rado Street
Architect: H.B. Copeland
Date Enacted: 4/17/90

Residence at 647 Escobar Avenue
Architect: H. George Fink Sr.
Date Enacted: 12/16/97

189

Residence at 1203 Ferdinand Street
Architect: John E. Pierson
Date Enacted: 5/13/97

Residence at 2114 Granada Boulevard
Located in the "Country Club of Coral Gables Historic District"
Architect: H. George Fink
Date Enacted: 1/8/91

Residence at 2123 Granada Boulevard
Architect: H. George Fink (Attribution)
Date Enacted: 6/22/94

Residence at 2214 Granada Boulevard
Architect: H. George Fink
Date Enacted: 4/12/94

Residence at 2616 Granada Boulevard
Architect: L.R. Patterson
Date Enacted: 7/8/97

Residence at 3018 Granada Boulevard
Architect: Alfred L. Klingbeil
Date Enacted: 10/14/97

Residence at 3603 Granada Boulevard
Architect: William Shanklin Jr.
Date Enacted: 8/29/95

Residence at 4200 Granada Boulevard
Architect: Phineas Paist (1948 alteration by H. George Fink)
Date Enacted: 2/14/95

Residence at 4501 Granada Boulevard
Architect: Phineas Paist
Date Enacted: 1/9/90

Residence at 1014 Lisbon Street
Architect: South Brandes
Date Enacted: 3/8/94

Residence at 2420 Madrid Street
Architect: Unknown
Date Enacted: 1/9/96

Residence at 916 Medina Avenue
Architect: Henry Hunter Jordan
Date Enacted: 8/26/97

Residence at 1314 Milan Avenue
Architect: E. Dean Parmelee
Date Enacted: 3/12/96

Residence at 4200 Monserrate Street
Architect: W. H. Baugh
Date Enacted: 6/22/94

Residence at 811 Navarre Avenue
Architect: Walter DeGarmo
Date Enacted: 2/11/97

Residence at 1141 North Greenway Drive
Located in the "Country Club of Coral Gables Historic District"
Architect: P. E. Robinson
Date Enacted: 2/9/93

Residence at 1205 Obispo Avenue
Architect: Walter DeGarmo
Date Enacted: 4/9/96

Residence at 1325 Obispo Avenue
Architect: Walter DeGarmo
Date Enacted: 6/13/95

Residence at 1328 Obispo Avenue
Architect: H. George Fink
Date Enacted: 1/9/96

Residence at 8021 Old Cutler Road
Architect: William Shanklin Jr.
Date Enacted: 3/13/95

Residence at 3612 Palmarito Street
Builder: Allan Artley Construction Company
Date Enacted: 3/12/96

Residence at 4855 Ponce de Leon Boulevard
Architect: D. L. Clarke
Date Enacted: 5/14/91

Residence at 215 Romano Avenue
Architect: H. George Fink
Date Enacted: 12/16/97

Residence at 222 Romano Avenue
Architect: H. George Fink
Date Enacted: 3/11/97

Residence at 1025 Sevilla Avenue
Architects: Phineas Paist and Harold D. Steward
Date Enacted: 2/13/96

Residence at 3317 Toledo Street
Architects: Phineas Paist and Harold D. Steward
Date Enacted: 2/17/98

Residence at 3505 Toledo Street
Architect: H. George Fink Sr.
Date Enacted: 7/16/96

Residence at 912 Valencia Avenue
Architect: Henry Vanderlyn
Date Enacted: 11/8/94

Santiago Street Historic District
810, 811, 814, 822, 832 and 910 Santiago Street
Architects: Various
Date Enacted: 6/11/96

Segovia Plaza
Intersection at Coral Way, Segovia Street, and North Greenway Drive
Designer: Denman Fink
Date Enacted: 8/30/88

Taylor Parks House
Residence at 1006 South Greenway Drive
Architect: Walter DeGarmo
Date Enacted: 10/12/82

Telefair Knight / Norman House
Residence at 4419 University Drive
Architects: J. Skinner and J. Pierson
Date Enacted: 10/10/78

The Chinese Village—Historic District—Residential District
5100, 5104, 5108, and 5112 Maggiore Street
534 Menendez Avenue
5125, 5129, and 5133 Riviera Drive
Architect: Henry Killam Murphy
Date Enacted: 7/22/86

The Church of the Little Flower Historic District
Bounded by Valencia Avenue, Palermo Avenue, Palos Street, and Indian Mound Trail
Architects: Gerald A. Barry; H. George Fink; Harold D. Steward; and Skinner
Date Enacted: 6/23/92

The Church of the Little Flower (Parish Hall)
Southeast Corner Anastasia Avenue, and Palermo Avenue
Architect: Gerald A. Barry
Date Enacted: 4/25/89

The Coliseum (Demolished 1993)
1500 Douglas Road
Architect: Arthur Ten Eyck Brown
Date Enacted: 11/8/88

The Country Club of Coral Gables Historic District
The area bounded by North and South Greenway Drives, surrounding and including Granada Golf Course
Architects: Multiple
Date Enacted: 2/14/89, 1/8/91, 2/9/93

The Florida Pioneer—Village Historic District
Residences at 4320, 4409, 4515, 4520, and 4620 Santa Maria Street
Architects: Skinner and Pierson
Date Enacted: 5/9/89

The French Country Village Historic District
Architects: Edgar Albright, Philip Goodwin, Frank Forster
Date Enacted: 2/27/90

The Gatekeeper's House—Fairchild Tropical Garden
10901 Old Cutler Road
Architect: William Lyman Phillips
Date Enacted: 10/11/84

The Italian Village Historic District
608, 625, 629, 633, and 644 Altara Avenue
4203, 4211, and 4301 Monserrate Street
4101, 4108, 4122, 4300, 4400, 4401, and 4408 Palmarito Street
631 San Esteban
641 San Lorenzo Avenue
Architects: A. K. Klingbeil; John and Coulton Skinner, R. F. Ware; and Robert Law Weed
Date Enacted: 6/23/92

The Miracle Theater
280 Miracle Mile
Architects: William H. Lee and Robert Collins
Date Enacted: 6/13/95

The Steven A. Ryan Residence
Residence at 3305 Alhambra Circle
Architect: Walter C. DeGarmo
Date Enacted: 9/23/86

The Venetia Apartments
2800 Toledo Street
Architect: Martin Hampton
Date Enacted: 9/6/88

Venetian Pool and Casino
Public / Recreational Boulevard
2701 De Soto Boulevard
Architects: Denman Fink and Phineas Paist
Date Enacted: 2/26/85

Warr Hoffman House
Residence at 1104 Malaga Avenue
Architect: H. George Fink
Date Enacted: 10/10/78

White Way Street Lights (Ornamental light fixtures)
University Drive, Anastasia Avenue, and Riviera Drive
Designers: Phineas Paist and Denman Fink
Date Enacted: 2/24/81

Zinsmaster Estate
House and Cottages at 1510 Madrid Street
Architects: William Bossman and E. Dean Parmalee
Date Enacted: 1/26/88

Bibliography

While I cite in the text numerous written works that were of great assistance in completing this project, I would like to call particular attention to the following:

Ashley, Kathryne. *George E. Merrick and Coral Gables, Florida.* Coral Gables: Crystal Bay, 1985.

Behar, Roberto M., and Maurice G. Culot, eds. *Coral Gables: An American Garden City.* Paris: Editions Norma, 1997.

The Biltmore Revisited. Coral Gables: Metropolitan Museum & Art Center, 1981.

LaRoue, Samuel D. Jr., and Ellen J. Uguccioni. *Coral Gables in Postcards.* Miami: Dade Heritage Trust, 1988.

Muir, Helen. *Miami, U.S.A.* 2nd ed. New York: Henry Holt, 1990.

Parks, Arva Moore. *Miami: The Magic City.* Miami: Centennial Press, 1991.

Roy, Joaquin. *The Streets of Coral Gables: Their Names and Meanings.* Coral Gables: University of Miami, 1989.

Zuckerman, Bertram. *The Dream Lives On: A History of the Fairchild Tropical Garden, 1938–1988.* Miami: Banyan Books, 1988.

—Les Standiford

Sponsors

Founder's Edition

Baptist Health Systems of South Florida

Merrick Edition

University of Miami

Chairman's Circle

The City of Coral Gables

Esslinger-Wooten-Maxwell Realtors

HealthSouth Doctors' Hospital

Lady Suzanna P. Tweed

President's Circle

BellSouth

The Biltmore Hotel

Coral Gables Lincoln Mercury

Republic National Bank

Robert L. Trescott, P.A.

Spillis Candela & Partners

*The Village of Merrick Park
A project of the Rouse Company*

Royal Palm Patrons
(see page 202)

Looking through the glass gallery section of the Miami Cardiac & Vascular Institute's interventional suites, visitors can view the control and procedure rooms. Its unique design allows physicians from around the world to observe and learn the procedures pioneered by Institute physicians. Patient privacy, of course, is easy as shutting the blinds. The Institute is an affiliate of Baptist Health Systems of South Florida.

Baptist Health Systems of South Florida

**BAPTIST HOSPITAL OF MIAMI ▪ SOUTH MIAMI HOSPITAL
BAPTIST CHILDREN'S HOSPITAL ▪ HOMESTEAD HOSPITAL
MARINERS HOSPITAL ▪ MIAMI CARDIAC & VASCULAR INSTITUTE**

Baptist Health Systems of South Florida is the region's largest not-for-profit health care organization, with 1,600 physicians (many with international reputations) and 7,000 employees serving 100,000 people annually. Headquartered in Coral Gables, the health system includes Baptist, Baptist Children's, South Miami, Homestead and Mariners Hospitals; Miami Cardiac & Vascular Institute; physicians' offices; and outpatient facilities. Patients benefit from the most advanced technology to treat cancer, serious childhood ailments, heart problems and other illnesses.

At the heart of the organization: its not-for-profit mission of service. Revenue above expenses goes to improving community health, with free or reduced-cost care for qualified residents, and free support groups, health education and screenings.

Baptist Health Systems of South Florida
6855 Red Road
Coral Gables, FL 33143
Phone: 305-273-2555
Fax: 305-273-2452

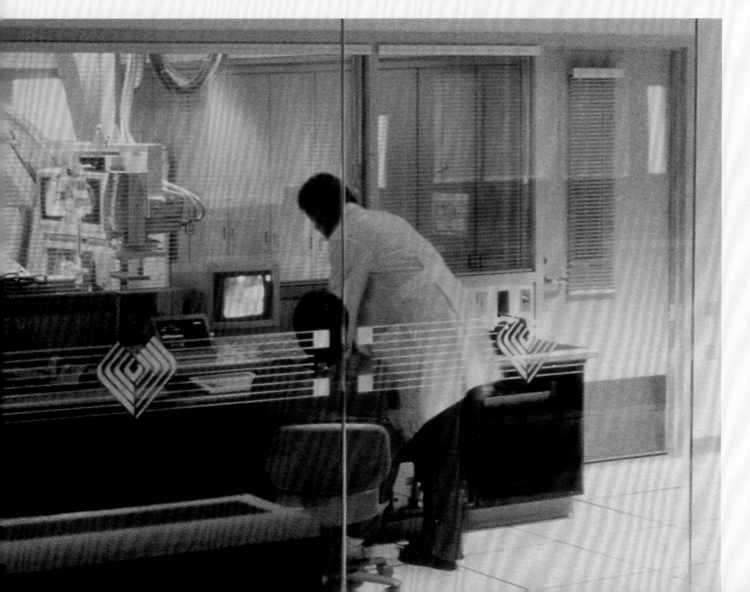

UNIVERSITY OF Miami

You cannot speak of Coral Gables without speaking of the University of Miami, the largest private research university in the southeastern United States.

Its presence in Coral Gables is measured in terms of history, numbers, and atmosphere. It is the second largest private employer in Miami-Dade County and has enriched the area through its cultural and educational offerings. Its history, dating back to a 1925 gift of land and cash by developer George E. Merrick, is inextricably tied with that of Coral Gables.

Currently entering its eighth decade of achievement, the University comprises 14 schools and colleges devoted to various fields of study from architecture to international studies. Nearly half of its 14,000 students are enrolled in graduate and professional programs, and the University today is ranked among the top 40 universities in the country.

The Coral Gables campus, with its two colleges and ten schools, is located on a lush 260-acre tract heavily utilized by members of the community. Other University of Miami campuses include the medical campus within the Jackson Memorial Medical Center complex, the Rosenstiel School of Marine and Atmospheric Science on Virginia Key and the South Campus, a research and development center 10 miles southwest of Coral Gables.

University of Miami
P. O. Box 248105
Coral Gables, FL 33124-4040
Phone: 305-284-5600
Fax: 305-284-2532

An initial $5 million investment by George Merrick has grown into an impressive campus mirroring academic excellence and tropical beauty.

The City of Coral Gables is committed to providing its residential and business population with the superior level of services that make Coral Gables one of the nation's most livable communities.

Emphasizing public safety and quality of life, the City boasts a Class 1 Fire Department and an internationally accredited Class 1 Police Department, as well as regionally and nationally recognized emergency management, recreation, public service, preservation, and construction regulation programs.

In addition, sound financial management allows the City to maintain one of the lowest millage rates in Miami-Dade County and ensures that the quality of services will continue.

City of Coral Gables
Columbus Center
One Alhambra Plaza, Suite 1110
Coral Gables, FL 33134
Phone: 305-460-5311
Fax: 305-445-9623

Esslinger-Wooten-Maxwell is a real estate company with a mission—to be of help. Personalized service has been both its motto and its strongest selling point since its formation in 1964 in what was then a sleepy tourist community. "Our emphasis has always been in the direction of service," says Ronald A. Shuffield, president.

Today, EWM is the first stop of major multinational corporations seeking relocation help as well as individuals seeking new homes. Its full-service offerings, all built on the company's solid foundation and reputation, include the sale and leasing of residential and commercial properties as well as property management.

Esslinger-Wooten-Maxwell Realtors
1360 South Dixie Highway
Coral Gables, FL 33146
Phone: 305-667-8871
Fax: 305-662-5646

HEALTHSOUTH
Doctors' Hospital

*H*EALTHSOUTH *Doctors' Hospital*, located in the heart of Coral Gables, is a 285-bed, acute-care facility delivering the highest standard of medical care. The hospital enjoys a reputation for excellence in patient care with medical specialties in orthopedics/sports medicine, state-of-the-art women's wellness center, technologically advanced operating suites, state-of-the-art radiologic imaging and obstetrics. In addition, HEALTHSOUTH Doctors' Hospital is committed to a mutually supportive relationship with our dedicated and highly qualified medical staff and other professionals to provide personalized, compassionate heathcare in our changing environment. In keeping with our nationally renowned Sports Medicine Program, HEALTHSOUTH Doctors' Hospital is proud to be the official Sports Medicine Provider for the Miami HEAT and the 1997 World Champion Florida Marlins.

HEALTHSOUTH Doctors' Hospital
5000 University Drive
Coral Gables, FL 33146
Phone: 305-666-2111
Fax: 305-662-4260

Lady Suzanna P. Tweed

*L*ady Suzanna P. Tweed has for many years been a giver of extraordinary gifts to her community, continuing a tradition of philanthropy initiated with her deceased husband, Carleton Tweed.

She has helped worthwhile causes, many of them devoted to benefitting children. In addition to the Museum of Science and Planetarium, she has both donated and helped raise funds for the Marian Center for disabled children and for the Camillus House for the homeless. Lady Tweed has been recognized repeatedly for her acts of generosity, including receiving the Gables Chamber of Commerce's Robert B. Knight Outstanding Citizen Award in 1984.

Lady Suzanna P. Tweed and
Carleton Tweed Charitable
Foundation, Inc.

⊕ **BELL**SOUTH®

*B*ellSouth (NYSE: BLS) is a $19 billion communications services company. It provides telecommunications, wireless communications, directory advertising and publishing, video, Internet, cable and information services to more than 27 million customers in twenty countries worldwide.

BellSouth
150 West Flagler Street, Suite 1820
Miami, FL 33130
Phone: 305-347-5458
Fax: 305-375-9311

*T*he grandeur of the past is clearly a part of the present at the Biltmore Hotel.

The hotel, built in 1926 as part of George Merrick's vision for the city, is today a four-star, four-diamond resort owned by Seaway Hotels Corporation. The 280 rooms and landscaped grounds—including the largest pool in the continental United States—seem a step back into the past, with all the amenities of modern life.

The Biltmore Hotel
1200 Anastasia Avenue
Coral Gables, FL 33134-6340
Phone: 305-445-1926
Fax: 305-913-3152

CORAL GABLES LINCOLN MERCURY

*C*oral Gables Lincoln Mercury has been family owned and operated since it opened January 10, 1954. Located at 4001 Ponce de Leon Boulevard, on six acres at the gateway to the Gables, it is a full-service dealership that prides itself on "giving people what they were promised."

Coral Gables Lincoln Mercury, Inc.
4001 Ponce de Leon Boulevard
Coral Gables, FL 33146
Phone: 305-445-7711
Fax: 305-445-5158

RNB REPUBLIC BANK

*R*epublic National Bank is one of South Florida's largest and strongest local banks. Founded in 1965, the bank has twenty-seven branches in Miami-Dade and Broward counties and offers customers a comprehensive range of products and services. It recently constructed a new fifteen-story corporate headquarters building in Coral Gables.

Republic National Bank of Miami
2800 Ponce de Leon Boulevard
Coral Gables, FL 33134
Phone: 305-441-7300
www.rnbmia.com

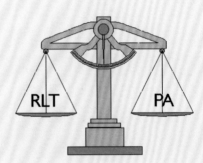

*R*obert L. Trescott's law firm specializes in taxation and estate planning. Mr. Trescott has been a part of the Coral Gables community since 1947, graduating from Coral Gables High in 1963. He earned his undergraduate and law degree from Florida State University, and his LL.M. in taxation from New York University. He is married to Cynthia and they have twin daughters, Allison and Chelsea.

Robert L. Trescott, PA
5351 Banya Drive
Coral Gables, FL 33156
Phone: 305-666-8360
Fax: 305-661-1913

Spillis Candela & Partners, Inc.
ARCHITECTURE/ENGINEERING/PLANNING/INTERIORS

*S*pillis Candela & Partners, a full-service architecture, engineering, planning, and interiors firm, provides market-focused professional services in Public/ Institutional, Education, Justice, Corporate, and Hospitality/Retail markets. SC&P is directed by thirteen partners and employs over two hundred fifty professionals. The firm is headquartered in Miami and maintains full-service offices in Orlando and Washington, D.C., as well as affiliate offices throughout Latin America.

Spillis Candela & Partners
800 Douglas Entrance
North Tower, Suite 200
Coral Gables, FL 33134-3119
Phone: 305-444-4691
Fax: 305-447-3566

THE VILLAGE of MERRICK PARK

A project of THE ROUSE COMPANY

*T*he Rouse Company's "Village of Merrick Park" continues the commercial and cultural renaissance of the Design District. It includes nationally recognized retailers Nordstrom's and Neiman Marcus, smaller retailers, residential apartments, a cinema, restaurants, and showroom space. These uses are organized on and about a public park providing an open and inviting environment respecting the scale, qua-lity, and urban character of Coral Gables while complementing the history that inspired George Merrick.

The Village of Merrick Park
2655 South Le Juene, Suite 514
Coral Gables, FL 33134
Phone: 305-441-1401
Fax: 305-445-0148

Royal Palm Patrons

Abood & Associates, Inc. / Donna Abood

Brooks Financial Corporation

The Calvin & Flavia Oak Foundation, Inc.

Colbert, Boue And Juncadella, C.P.A.'s

Esso Inter-America, Inc.

Home Financing Center

Lane Computer Solutions

Ligne Roset

Louis Dreyfus Property Group

Northern Trust Bank of Florida, N.A.

Prudential Florida Realty Coral Gables Office / Nancy Barreto Hogan

Robert J. Fewell Company

Sharff Wittmer Kurtz & Jackson, P.A., Certified Public Accountants

Don, Jeannett, Kathleen & Donald Slesnick

SunTrust Bank Miami, N.A.

Terryfic Ad Specialties, Inc. / Kathy Terry

Photo Credits

Baptist Health Systems of South Florida — 170, 171, 194

Biltmore Hotel — 44

Contreras, Don —18

Coral Gables, City of — 5, 21 (bottom), 22, 29, 34 (bottom), 35, 36, 41, 45, 46, 50 (bottom), 50 (bottom), 68, 70 (bottom), 72, 75, 80, 82, 83, 84 (insets), 86, 87, 88, 89, 90, 91, 92, 94, 95, 100, 102, 104, 105, 108, 110, 112, 116, 117, 118, 119, 120 (bottom), 122, 123, 124, 126, 128, 130, 132, 138 (top), 141, 144, 146, 148, 149, 167, 169, 192

Hawkins, Ken — front endsheet, 2, 6, 8, 12, 14, 17, 20, 27 (top), 28 (bottom), 30, 32, 54, 64, 65 (top), 67, 71 (inset), 76, 77 (bottom), 78, 79, 96, 97, 114, 134, 135, 136, 138 (center), 140, 142, 156, 160, 172, 173 (bottom), 174, 175 (all), 180, 181 (all), 182, 183 (bottom), 184, 186, 208

HealthSouth Doctors' Hospital — 173 (top)

Kennedy, Brenda Ann — 52

Landis, Richard — 158

LaRoue Jr., Samuel D. — A special appreciation for providing the post-card photos on 18, 19, 34, 50, 70 (top), 77 (top), 81, 121 (top), 131 (bottom), 155 (top)

Maltz, Alan — 10, 16, 24, 25, 27 (bottom), 28 (top), 38, 38, 40, 60 (top), 55, 56, 59 (top), 62, 66, 73 (bottom), 74, 84 (top & bottom), 98, 101, 143, 147, 150, 152, 166, 168, 175, 179, 183 (top)

Messerschmidt, Al — 159

Portnoy, Daniel — 23, 42, 52 (bottom), 71, 106 (all), 178, back endsheet

Starr, Steve — 62

University of Miami — 48, 154, 162, 163, 164, 196

University of Miami: Ibis Yearbook (1953) — 49, 155

Index